18, 25-32

Judicial Administration
The American Experience

Judicial Administration
The American Experience

by

DELMAR KARLEN

*Director of the Institute of Judicial
Administration Inc., New York, and
Professor of Law, New York University*

*Published under the auspices of the Institute
of Judicial Administration in the University
of Birmingham*

LONDON
BUTTERWORTHS
1970

ENGLAND:	BUTTERWORTH & CO. (PUBLISHERS) LTD. LONDON: 88 Kingsway, WC2B 6AB
AUSTRALIA:	BUTTERWORTH & CO. (AUSTRALIA) LTD. SYDNEY: 20 Loftus Street MELBOURNE: 343 Little Collins Street BRISBANE: 240 Queen Street
CANADA:	BUTTERWORTH & CO. (CANADA) LTD. TORONTO: 14 Curity Avenue, 374
NEW ZEALAND:	BUTTERWORTH & CO. (NEW ZEALAND) LTD. WELLINGTON: 49/51 Ballance Street AUCKLAND: 35 High Street
SOUTH AFRICA:	BUTTERWORTH & CO. (SOUTH AFRICA) (PTY.) LTD. DURBAN: 33/35 Beach Grove

ISBN 0 406 60900 4

PRINTED IN GREAT BRITAIN
AT THE ST ANN'S PRESS, PARK ROAD, ALTRINCHAM

Foreword

by

The Honourable Warren E. Burger

Chief Justice of the United States

Professor Karlen's lectures, originally delivered to an audience of English judges, lawyers and law students, deserve a counterpart American audience perhaps even more. They present what is sadly lacking in legal literature today—an overview of the administration of justice and of its 'engineers', the lawyers. It covers criminal as well as civil, state as well as federal courts, and a comparative analysis of the workings of the system from which ours springs.

The picture is not pretty, but neither is the subject it depicts. Nor were earlier pictures of the same subject painted by Roscoe Pound and Arthur T. Vanderbilt. This book is in their tradition, which is not surprising from an author who is Director of the organization they helped establish to carry on their battle for better courts. Pound was in large part the inspiration and Vanderbilt the first President of the Institute of Judicial Administration. Pound was on its original Board of Fellows.

Professor Karlen's admiration for the English system is not concealed; he finds the American system markedly deficient by comparison. He challenges us with this paradox: England has far fewer judges and lawyers; nevertheless, it disposes of its cases far more rapidly, and with far greater public satisfaction. How can this be? He suggests not a single, simple answer, but a variety of partial answers—different conceptions of the function of judges, partly stemming from the absence of a written constitution and the lack of a 'judicial supremacy' doctrine as a source of power to nullify an act of Parliament (hence, in England there are no cases like *Brown* v. *Board of Education* or *Baker* v. *Carr*); different ideas about *stare decisis* and *res judicata* (thus in England, overrulings are infrequent and there are no post conviction remedies); different methods of public participation in the judicial process (lay magistrates in England as against our grand and petit juries); different methods of criminal prosecution and defense (England has no counterpart to our 'district attorneys' and indigent 'legal aid' service, like the prosecution function, is assigned to practicing barristers). These are but a few of the many contrasts between the two legal systems explored in this book; they can hardly fail to stimulate American judges and lawyers to think more deeply about our own ways of administering justice. Readers may or may not agree with the author about the virtues of the English system as compared to our own, but I suspect that few will close the book with any feeling that there is nothing more to be learned from England; as indeed, England has learned some important lessons from the Napoleonic Code systems of Europe, notably by eliminating the use of juries in all but a few kinds of civil cases.

Comparative aspects aside, this book covers a surprising range of subjects which are not traditionally encompassed within the scope of judicial administration—legal education, federalism, judicial supremacy, substantive law reform, contingent fees in civil cases, and the publication of only carefully selected appellate opinions, to mention a few. These seemingly disparate topics are seldom considered in relation to each other or in relation to the traditional staples of judicial administration—selection, tenure, retirement and removal of judges, court structure, etc.—but in combination they deeply affect the quality of justice. They deserve consideration in a book on judicial administration. Karlen's definition of judicial administration is broad enough to cover all that affects the total functioning of the courts.

One matter affecting the operation of a judicial system of special significance to judges is their own attitude in deciding individual cases. Do they think only of the particular litigants before them to the exclusion of the impact of their decisions on the total functioning of the system? English judges and lawyers wonder about cases like *Mapp* v. *Ohio, Duncan* v. *Louisiana, Townsend* v. *Sain,* and *Fay* v. *Noia.* A reminder that judges should be conscious of how their own decisions may contribute to delay, congestion and crisis in the courts ought not to be necessary, but unfortunately it is. English judges think of both cases and the system. Judicial administration, after all, does not depend exclusively upon legislative appropriations, techniques of calendaring, clerical help, physical facilities, or electronic data processing. It depends in part upon judges themselves being aware of how their decisions in individual cases may affect the total functioning of the courts. If a judicial system is malfunctioning, it is not always or solely because of factors beyond the control of the judges themselves. English judges use a form of rulemaking, the 'judges' rules', which avoids the internal frictions and confusion engendered by trying to formulate rules of procedure on a case-by-case basis. In our system, the 'prospective only' doctrine had to be devised to make some of our new constitutional doctrines more palatable.

Another factor noted by Professor Karlen is the high standards of the English barrister, not only in terms of extraordinary professional advocacy but in ethics and courtroom decorum—civility, that indispensable lubricant to the litigation process. Through the Bar Council and the Senate of the four Inns of Court, strict adherence to standards of ethics and decorum are maintained. I say maintained because discipline rarely needs enforcement in the coercive or penal sense. Barristers know the rules, all judges are former barristers and everyone realizes that a breach of rules will bring disaster, professionally. The bar of this country by comparison seems almost anarchic when compared with the profession in England. That the British can maintain these high standards and yet have what is uniformly the most vigorous and effective advocacy ever developed demonstrates the compatability of zeal and ethics in the law.

As a long time colleague of Professor Karlen in the Institute of Judicial Administration and in summer work at the New York University Law School, I might be accused of a bias in his favor. I think I have none. We simply see these problems in much the same light.

I can heartily commend his work to every member of the American legal community.

Foreword

by

Sir George Coldstream,

K.C.B., K.C.V.O., Q.C.

Honorary Reader in Judicial Administration in the University of Birmingham;
Formerly Permanent Secretary to the Lord Chancellor and Clerk of the
Crown in Chancery

I believe that Professor Karlen's three lectures published in this book will be found interesting and instructive not only by lawyers and students of law but by the increasing number of people in all walks of life who want to know more about how justice is administered in America. I hope I am right in this belief because I have to admit to a small measure of responsibility for their content. Before deciding on the general plan of his lectures Professor Karlen asked me what features of the American scene were most likely to prove informative and entertaining for British audiences. I urged him not to assume any high degree of pre-knowledge in those attending his lectures because, apart from some specialists to whom his subject is already familiar, I knew from personal experience how superficial is the understanding possessed by most of us in England about the American constitutional and judicial systems. With some hesistation Professor Karlen accepted this advice, and so it is that these lectures range over the whole constitutional and institutional framework within which American justice has to operate.

Professor Karlen writes of the 'unblinking self-criticism' which Americans, lawyers and laymen alike, direct to all aspects of their system of judicial administration, a term which is intended to include everything involved in making criminal and civil justice available to the community. Until recently I doubt whether self-criticism has been a notable feature of the British lawyer's attitude to his system. As the inheritors of long traditions and old established institutions we have been rather slow to appreciate the value of research into comparative methods and processes overseas. We have been content to accept impressions of American justice from films and novels and from reports of notorious but un-typical trials which have made the headlines. Now that some features of our own system are under strain, particularly the mounting numbers of criminal cases to be handled by the courts, we should do well to realise that America has been grappling with these problems for a long while and at least to look at the various ways in which they have tried, and are trying, to deal with them.

I think that many lawyers and students may be dismayed at the report which Professor Karlen gives of some features of the current situation in America. I do not wish to cast myself in the role of Cassandra but I suggest that it would be foolish for us in England to ignore the warning signs, to assume 'that it cannot happen here' and that the traditional English judicial systems will always be capable of taking the strain whatever the volume and complexity of the business to be handled by our courts and judges.

One of the objectives of both the American and English Institutes of Judicial Administration is to foster research into all aspects of the administration of justice. Thus we hope to benefit the cause of justice in both countries in the belief that each may learn from the other. But research alone will avail us little; we have to convey to politicians and lawyers and the interested public the need for reforms and to suggest practical methods of achieving them. The valuable work done over the last sixteen years by the American Institute and its recognised place among American legal institutions is a great encouragement to the recently formed English Institute which is attached to the Law Faculty of the University of Birmingham. Professor Karlen's experience in this field is probably unrivalled in his country. I think that everyone who reads these lectures will realise that the broad brush with which he has chosen to paint the scene conceals a mastery of detail of all aspects of judicial administration in America. I commend them to all in England and Wales who care for the maintenance of high standards in the administration of justice.

Preface

This book contains, in revised and updated form, the substance of three lectures delivered in England in December 1968 upon the occasion of the founding of the English Institute of Judicial Administration at the University of Birmingham. The first lecture was given at University College in the University of London, and the last two at the Law Faculty of the University of Birmingham.

Conscious that I was being invited to carry coals to Newcastle, I decided that the only proper approach was to be completely uninhibited in describing the American system, 'warts and all.' Only by being frank about American weaknesses as well as strengths, shortcomings as well as achievements, could I hope to help the English discover what, if anything, they might wish to borrow from American experience. Only in that way could I help them see their own system in a new light and reconsider values which they might be inclined to overlook or take for granted. So I decided to follow the advice of today's angry young men and 'tell it like it is.' I even tried to give a living demonstration of one of the techniques of judicial reform in which Americans specialize—namely, unblinking self-criticism.

While this book deals primarily with judicial administration in the United States, it is also a comparative Anglo-American study. It contains a running comparison, sometimes explicit, always at least implicit, between the administration of justice in the United States and that in England.

Delmar Karlen

December 15, 1969

Contents

Chapter 1   *The Machinery of Justice in the United States*

Before undertaking to describe judicial administration in the United States, I should try to define the subject matter. 'Judicial Administration' is not a word of art with a settled meaning, but I think it can fairly be said to cover, as the Lord Chancellor of England said in his 1968 Holdsworth lecture, all of the activities that go on behind the scenes of any real-life courtroom drama. As he pointed out, when a spectator walks into a courtroom, he sees the judge, the advocates, a witness or two, perhaps a dozen jurors, each person playing an assigned role; the spectator does not think much, if at all, about how the scene before him came into being—how the man presiding became a judge, why the case is being tried in this court rather than another one, how the jurors were chosen, whose responsibility it was to see that the courtroom was available and that the bailiffs, ushers, clerks and reporters were present, who determines the pay of the judge and other personnel of the court—but somebody has to think about such questions. Those who do are concerned with judicial administration. They are like the producer of a theatrical performance, without whose efforts the show simply could not go on. While some people define judicial administration as covering only the housekeeping management of the courts, I am using the term in a much broader sense—to cover court structure, judicial selection, the training and organization of the legal profession, and in general, all of the elements which go into making a judicial system good or bad.

B

In this chapter, I shall deal with matters fundamental to an understanding of American justice, particularly the effect of a federal system of government and the impact of a written constitution.

American legal institutions are derived from those in England. That explains why the two systems are alike in such fundamental matters as a common conception of the rule of law and in basically similar conceptions of the rights, duties, liberties and privileges of individual citizens. It is not, however, a sufficient explanation of why the two systems are as different as they are. To understand the differences, we must remind ourselves that the American legal system is separated from the English legal system by about 300 years of historical development.

When in the 17th century English colonists came to North America, they brought with them the legal institutions they had known at home, and transplanted them into new soil. The seeds took root and flourished, ultimately driving out alien growths which had been imported from other cultures by settlers coming from other nations.

Each colony, however, was a separate entity. It was subject to some control from London, of course, but it also enjoyed a considerable measure of local autonomy. Its laws and legal institutions could and did develop distinct, individual patterns. The statutes enacted in Massachusetts were not necessarily the same as those enacted in Virginia; and the courts of Maryland did not necessarily operate in the same way as the courts of Delaware. There was no central government of the colonies in North America to insist upon uniformity, and not even much communication between the separate colonies. Even the common law of England, which was accepted by all of the colonies and which might have been expected to be the same everywhere, did not achieve uniformity. In a relatively short time it became fragmented into the common law of New York, the common law of Connecticut, the common law of Rhode Island, and so forth. The common law received from England had within itself the seeds of growth and change, so that each new judicial decision made it a little bit different than it had ever been before. Judges in one colony, knowing little, if anything, about decisions being made by judges in other colonies, and in any event not being bound by those decisions, decided cases according to their own best judgment, interpreting and transforming the common law. Inevitably, different rules of substantive and procedural law and different standards of judicial administration developed in the several colonies.

In the last quarter of the eighteenth century, the colonies united and formed a new nation. The structure they created, however, was not a unitary government like that which prevails in England. It was a federal government—an entirely different thing. The colonies became states and retained many of their former powers. So substantial were those powers that some states began to think of themselves and to call themselves 'sovereign' states, thus coining for later generations of political orators a catch phrase that they seem to find irresistible even today. The 'sovereignty' so asserted was far from complete, for the new central government was given control over external affairs and over some domestic affairs as well, such as currency, the postal service and interstate commerce.[1] The states were prohibited from interfering with the operation of the central government, as by closing their borders, or raising their own armies or setting up tariff barriers, or establishing their own systems of coinage, but otherwise they retained most of the powers of government. They were free to regulate activities within their own borders and to establish such courts, legislative bodies and executive agencies as they saw fit.[2]

This allocation of powers as between the federal and the state governments was embodied in a written constitution, and for that reason, if no other, it remains substantially unchanged today—at least formally. About 70 years after the formation of the federal government, when our civil war was concluded, the Constitution was amended to prohibit the states from

[1] U.S. Const. art. I, §8.
[2] U.S. Const. amend. X.

depriving any citizen, black or white, of due process of law or of the equal protection of the laws,[1] but otherwise the powers of the states were not constitutionally curtailed. As we all know, however, the powers of the federal government, thanks to history, Presidential leadership, Congress and the Supreme Court, are immensely greater today than could have been foreseen by the framers of the Constitution. Nevertheless, no matter how powerful and far reaching the federal government is, it still has only such powers as are vested in it by the Constitution as interpreted by the Supreme Court of the United States.[2] 'States' rights', about which one hears so much in political oratory, are still very much alive.

As a result, the laws and legal institutions of the United States still exhibit the same diversity that prevailed in colonial times. Perhaps even greater diversity, for law in the several states has had to adapt itself to large populations of immensely varied ethnic and cultural backgrounds. The problems of New York are assuredly not the same as those of Wyoming. There is no such thing as national criminal law or a national law of torts or property. If you should ask what the American law on gambling is or what are the American grounds for divorce, no one could tell you—or at least not simply and quickly. He would have to explain instead the gambling and divorce laws of 50 different states. What is true of statutory law is also true of judge-made law. The courts of California are not bound by the decisions of courts in New York or any other state. There is no such thing as a national common law, not even in the federal courts.

Nevertheless, there are forces working toward uniformity. Judges often cite cases from other states, not because they are controlling precedents, but because they are the products of a common judicial tradition, and deal with basically similar problems. Statutes are freely copied from state to state. In areas where uniformity is especially important, like the law

---

[1] U.S. Const. amend. XIV.

[2] I. B. Schwartz, *A Commentary on the Constitution of the U.S.* 88 (1963).

of negotiable instruments, identical state statutes are enacted;[1] and in areas where cooperation between the states is necessary, as in the interstate extradition of felons, reciprocal statutes are enacted, thanks largely to the efforts of an organization of state representatives known as the Commissioners on Uniform Laws.[2] Law schools take students from all over the country, and concentrate their studies on legal principles of general application rather than on the rules prevailing in a single state. Writers and publishers produce textbooks, treatises, digests and encyclopedias aimed at a national market. Lawyers from all states join together in the American Bar Association and other national organizations to protect professional interests throughout the nation and to work toward improvement in the law generally. Because of these various forces and others to be mentioned later, there is at least some coherence and unity in the separate systems in the 50 states.

STATE COURTS

Since each state is free to establish its own judicial system, it is not surprising that court structure varies from state to state. In some states jurisdiction is fragmented between a great many different courts with little or no centralized administration, while in others it is concentrated in a few courts subject to strong administrative control. Nevertheless, because of the essential similarity of judicial business everywhere, a general pattern can can be discerned.[3]

At the base of the judicial pyramid in each state are likely to be a large number of tribunals organized on a local basis, handling

[1] E.g., the Uniform Commercial Code, encompassing nine articles which cover the entire spectrum of commercial transactions, has been adopted, with minor variations, in forty-nine of the fifty states (Louisiana is the only state which has failed to adopt the Code).

[2] E.g., the Uniform Criminal Extradition Act. Approximately 120 Uniform and Model Acts have been recommended for adoption by the various states. See, *Uniform Laws Annotated*, vols. 1–10.

[3] See generally, D. Karlen, *The Citizen in Court*, Chs. 1–7 (1964); R. Pound, *Organization of Courts*, Ch. VII (1940); Institute of Judicial Administration (hereinafter abbreviated I.J.A.), *A Guide to Court Systems* (4th ed. 1966).

small civil claims where the amount in controversy is strictly limited, and small criminal cases where the maximum penalties are strictly limited. These are very rough equivalents of the English magistrate courts and county courts. Above these are trial courts empowered to handle more serious criminal cases and larger civil cases. In some states they have probate and juvenile jurisdiction as well, while in other states separate courts are established for those purposes. These general trial courts are fewer in number than the inferior courts and are usually organized on a regional basis, sometimes with judges holding court in several cities. Such courts are the rough equivalents—again very rough—of the English High Court, following basically similar procedures except for the fact that they use civil juries more extensively.

Finally, at the top of each state system is a single supreme court, usually empowered to hear both civil and criminal appeals. It is the rough equivalent of the English Court of Appeal. In the more populous states where the volume of litigation is high, intermediate appellate courts may be sandwiched between the trial courts and the state supreme court. Where such courts exist, appeal to them is ordinarily as of right, and further appeals to the state supreme court are ordinarily allowed only in the discretion of that court. American appellate courts at all levels perform the same functions as English appellate courts, but their procedures are markedly different. I shall discuss these procedures when we reach the Supreme Court of the United States.

However judicial work may be distributed between the various courts in a state, their combined jurisdiction is very extensive. They have exclusive power to try criminal prosecutions arising out of violations of their own state laws. Since most crimes are defined by state rather than federal law, this means that state courts handle the overwhelming bulk of all criminal prosecutions in the nation. They do not handle prosecutions arising under the laws of sister states or under federal laws. In civil matters, state courts handle not only claims based upon their own laws, but also those based upon the laws of sister states. That is because most civil actions are transitory, and because the courts of each state are required by the Federal Constitution to give 'full faith and credit' to the laws of sister states.¹ Finally, state courts can and must handle claims created by federal law.² The so-called 'supremacy clause' of the Federal Constitution provides that:

> 'This Constitution, and the Laws of the United States which shall be made in Pursuance thereof; and all Treaties made, or which shall be made, under the Authority of the United States, shall be the supreme Law of the Land; and the Judges in any State shall be bound thereby; any thing in the Constitution or Laws of any State to the Contrary notwithstanding.'³

Because of this clause, state courts in appropriate cases are required to interpret federal statutes, sometimes even to hold them invalid as violating the Federal Constitution. They are also required in appropriate cases to invalidate their own state laws, sometimes even provisions in their own state constitutions, when they conflict with the Federal Constitution or with valid federal laws made under its authority. All such decisions, as I shall explain more fully later, are subject to ultimate review in the Supreme Court of the United States.

FEDERAL COURTS

Paralleling the court systems of the 50 states, or perhaps one might say superimposed upon them, is a separate system of federal courts, making 51 systems in all.

For purposes of federal jurisdiction at the trial court level, the nation is divided geographically into about 90 districts in such a way that the more populous states have two to four districts within their borders, while the more sparsely settled states have only one. In each district there is a tribunal known as a Federal 'District Court'.⁴ It is a trial court, operating on the same level as the state trial courts. Unlike them, however, the Federal District Court is a court of specialized jurisdiction. The only

¹ U.S. Const. art. IV. § 1.
² *Second Employers' Liability Cases*, 223 U.S. 1 (1911).
³ U.S. Const. art. IV.
⁴ 28 U.S. §§ 81–144.

criminal cases it can try are those arising out of the violation of federal criminal laws, and over these it has exclusive jurisdiction.[1] Because of the restricted powers of the federal government, however, there are relatively few such cases compared to the number of criminal cases tried in state courts, and they concern mainly narcotics, smuggling, mail robberies, income tax evasions, treason, espionage and other out-of-the-ordinary crimes. Federal power to define crime, however, is more extensive than these examples would suggest. Under the Interstate and Foreign Commerce clause of the Constitution, the federal government can enact legislation which reaches activities crossing state boundaries.[2] Thus the Mann Act prohibits the transportation of women across state lines for purposes of prostitution[3] and the Lindbergh Law makes kidnapping a federal crime if the victim is carried across state lines.[4] Furthermore, under Congress' power to impose taxes, individuals who have committed state crimes, whether prosecuted for them or not, can be prosecuted under federal law in federal courts if they fail to pay federal taxes on their ill-gotten gains.[5] Because of the ability of Congress to define crimes in connection with its regulation of interstate commerce, its power to impose taxes, and other limited, yet vitally important powers, the United States Department of Justice is able to lead the attack on organized crime throughout the nation. Nevertheless, the fact remains that most common crimes like assault, murder, robbery and rape are state offenses tried by state courts. Thus, when President Kennedy was assassinated in Dallas, Texas in 1963, his killer, had he lived, would have had to be tried in a state court of Texas, for he had committed no federal crime. Since then Congress has enacted legislation which makes the assassination of the President a

---

[1] 18 U.S.C. § 3231.

[2] U.S. Const. art. I § 8.

[3] 18 U.S.C. § 2421.

[4] 18 U.S.C. § 1201.

[5] *James* v. *U.S.*, 366 U.S. 213 (1961).

federal crime, and also covers such closely related crimes as a conspiracy to assassinate the President-Elect.[1]

The civil jurisdiction of federal district courts is also relatively narrow. They are limited by constitutional and statutory provisions to two main types of cases—those arising under federal laws and those involving citizens of different states.[2] The cases based on federal law are limited in number because of the restricted legislative power of Congress which I have already mentioned. They are further limited by a requirement which applies to some but not all cases, that they must involve $10,000 or more in controversy.[3] They are still further limited as a practical matter by the fact that state courts have concurrent jurisdiction with the federal courts over almost all such cases. Just because a case is based upon federal law does not mean that it must be brought in a federal court. It can equally well be brought in a state court. There are some exceptions where Congress has vested exclusive jurisdiction in federal courts over certain types of litigation, such as admiralty cases,[4] patent and copyright matters[5] and claims against the federal government,[6] but these specialties do not bulk large in the total litigation of the nation.

Diversity of citizenship cases—those involving citizens of different states—account for about one half of the civil cases between private parties in the federal district courts. All of these must involve $10,000 or more in controversy,[7] and all are equally within the competence of state courts. Indeed, when a federal court is handling such a case, it is acting as if it were just another court of the state in which it is sitting. The case is based upon state substantive law and there is no federal substantive law to be applied, not even federal common law.[8] At one time, federal

---

[1] 18 U.S.C. § 1751 (1964).
[2] U.S. Const. art. III. § 2; 28 U.S.C. §§ 1331 and 1332.
[3] 28 U.S.C. § 1331.
[4] 28 U.S.C. § 1333.
[5] 28 U.S.C. § 1338.
[6] 28 U.S.C. § 1346.
[7] 28 U.S.C. § 1332.
[8] *Erie Railroad Co.* v. *Tompkins*, 304 U.S. 64 (1938).

judges acted as if there were a national body of common law.[1] This was when the legal profession believed or professed to believe that judges did not make law, and that the common law, to use Justice Holmes' phrase, was some sort of 'brooding omnipresence in the sky.'[2] In it were rules to fit every conceivable situation and all that judges had to do was study it long enough and hard enough to discover the rule that would fit the case at hand and then apply it. Federal judges, of course, considered themselves just as capable as state judges at this game, and therefore did not consider themselves bound to follow state court decisions. They sometimes reached conclusions contrary to those reached in the state courts. The consequence was that the result in a given case might depend upon whether it was tried in a state court or a federal court. This went on for about a hundred years until finally in 1938 the Supreme Court of the United States put a stop to it. It rejected the view that it held earlier about a 'brooding omnipresence in the sky' in place of the more realistic view that the common law was nothing more nor less than the sum total of judicial decisions at a given time in a particular set of courts. Thus there was a common law of New York formed by the decisions of its courts, and a common law of Pennsylvania formed by the decisions of its courts, but there was no general common law existing outside of the states yet obligatory within them. Having gone this far, the Supreme Court went on to recognize that it, along with the lower federal courts, had been following an unconstitutional course of conduct in presuming to lay down rules of general law which would have been beyond the power of Congress to enact. It held that henceforth the federal courts, except in matters governed by the Federal Constitution or by treaties or Acts of Congress, were to apply state law, whether it was legislatively enacted or judicially declared.[3]

---

[1] *Swift* v. *Tyson*, 16 Pet. 1 (1842).

[2] Holmes, J., dissenting in *Southern Pacific Co.* v. *Johnson*, 244 U.S. 205, 222 (1917); *Black & White Taxicab and Transfer Co.* v. *Brown and Yellow Taxicab and Transfer Co.*, 276 U.S. 518 (1928). See also, Clark, 'The Brooding Omnipresence of *Erie Railroad Co.* v. *Tompkins*', 55 Yale L. J. 267 (1946).

[3] *Erie Railroad Co.* v. *Tompkins*, *supra* p. 9, n.8

From what I have been saying about the limited jurisdiction of the federal district courts, one can readily see that they are not the basic trial courts of the nation, but specialized tribunals handling a comparatively small volume of business. The judges think that their volume of business is enormous, and it is by English standards, but not by American state standards. There are only 334 federal trial judges[1] as against about 800 state trial judges in New York alone,[2] not counting justices of the peace. The basic trial courts, the essential ones, are those of the states. They can handle most cases which are within the competence of the federal district courts, plus a great many more beyond their competence. Relatively few cases are based upon federal law and relatively few involve citizens of different states, or for that matter more than $10,000 in controversy. The great majority of cases are based upon state law and involve only citizens of the same state. These are exclusively within the jurisdiction of state courts.

Above the district courts in the federal hierarchy are United States Courts of Appeals. There are eleven such courts, organized on a geographical basis, one for each circuit into which the nation is divided.[3] Each circuit except for that of the District of Columbia covers several states and consequently a fairly large number of federal judicial districts. These Courts of Appeals occupy the same position in relation to the district courts within the circuits as state supreme courts occupy in relation to the lower courts of their respective states. They have no power to hear appeals from state courts even within their own circuits. Neither are their decisions binding precedents for those courts.[4] Their only binding effect is on the federal trial courts within their respective circuits. In other words, a decision of the United States Court of Appeals for the Second Circuit, embracing the

[1] 28 U.S.C. § 133; see also, *Annual Report of the Director of the Administrative Office of the United States Courts*, 1968, 90.
[2] *Thirteenth Annual Report of the Judicial Conference of the State of New York* 318 (1968); New York Law Journal, vol. 159, no. 102, p. 1, cols. 7, 8.
[3] 28 U.S.C. §§ 41–48.
[4] *State* v. *Coleman*, 46 N. J. 16 at 35–38, 214 A.2d 393, at 403–404 (1965).

states of New York, Connecticut and Vermont, is not binding on a federal court sitting in Boston, Massachusetts.[1] Up to this level, it is apparent that the federal courts are parallel to the state courts, not above them. A case which is tried in a state court is appealed to a higher state court, not to any federal court; and a case tried in a federal court is appealed to a higher federal court, not to any state court. One seeming exception must be mentioned, and it is an important one. After a criminal case has been tried in a state court and appealed up through the state hierarchy, and after all post-conviction remedies within the state system have been exhausted, the defendant can still bring what is colloquially and confusingly called a 'habeas corpus' proceeding in a federal district court before a single trial judge to inquire into the legality of his detention.[2] The theory is that state courts which violate the constitutional rights of the accused thereby forfeit jurisdiction. If the defendant loses in the district court, he can appeal its judgment up through the federal hierarchy of courts. It is not surprising that some state judges feel offended by this strange procedure.

THE SUPREME COURT OF THE UNITED STATES

Above the United States Courts of Appeals and also above the supreme courts of the various states is a unique tribunal— the Supreme Court of the United States. It is the highest court of the nation and certainly the most powerful, but its jurisdiction is specialized. It does not have power to review the decisions of state courts generally, but only those which involve questions of federal law of controlling importance.[3] If a state supreme court were to change a common law rule or interpret a state statute or hold a state statute invalid as violating

---

[1] *Banana Distributors, Inc.* v. *United Fruit Co.*, 27 F.R.D. 403 (S.D. N.Y. 1961); *Welp* v. *U.S.*, 103 F. Supp. 551 (D.C. Iowa 1955) reversed on other grounds, 201 F.2d 128 (8th Cir. 1953).

[2] 28 U.S.C. §§ 2241, 2254. For a general discussion of post-conviction procedures, see, Mayers, 'Federal Review of State Convictions: The Need for Procedural Reappraisal', 34 Geo. Wash. L. Rev. 615 (1966); American Bar Association Project, *Standards Relating to Post-Conviction Remedies* (1967).

[3] 28 U.S.C. § 1257; Sup. Ct. R. 15 (1) (e); *Lynch* v. *New York ex rel. Pierson*, 293 U.S. 52 (1934).

the state constitution, its decision would not be subject to review in the Supreme Court of the United States. On all such issues the state supreme court is the court of last resort. Thus if the Supreme Court of California were to abolish the defense of contributory negligence in tort actions in California, the Supreme Court of the United States would be powerless to prevent it. On the other hand, if the state supreme court were to interpret a federal statute or hold either a federal or state statute invalid as violating the Federal Constitution, the case would present a federal question of controlling importance.[1] For that reason, further review in the Supreme Court of the United States would be possible. The same general principles apply to decisions of lower federal courts. Theoretically all such decisions are reviewable,[2] but unless they present federal questions of the same type I have been describing, the Supreme Court of the United States has no function to perform.

Even when an important federal question is presented, however, review in the Supreme Court ordinarily is not mandatory.[3] For the most part, review is discretionary with the Court itself, as indeed it almost has to be in view of the fact that there are 61 appellate courts (50 state supreme courts and 11 federal courts of appeals) from which cases may come, not to mention a variety of lower courts from which direct appeals lie in special circumstances.[4] When a litigant seeks review by the Supreme Court, he

[1] 28 U.S.C. § 1247; *New York* v. *O'Neill*, 359 U.S. 1 (1958).

[2] 28 U.S.C. §§ 1252–1254.

[3] Sup. Ct. R. 19 (1); See also, T. Clark, 'The Supreme Court Conference', 19 F.R.D. 303 (1956); 'Chief Justice Hughes in Defense of the Court', March 21, 1937, Senate Report 711, 75th Cong. 1st Sess. 38–40 (1937); and Chief Justice Vinson's Speech to the A.B.A. Sept. 7, 1949, quoted in D. Karlen, *Primer of Procedure* 110 (1952).

[4] Direct appeals to the Supreme Court from decisions of District Courts lie from: decisions invalidating Acts of Congress, 28 U.S.C. § 1252; decisions of three-judge courts, 28 U.S.C. § 1253; in criminal cases involving the validity of construction of a statute upon which an indictment or information is founded, 18 U.S.C. § 3731; and in every civil action brought in any district court of the United States under any of the commerce, trade, or transportation acts wherein the United States is complainant, 15 U.S.C. § 29 and 49 U.S.C. § 45. Direct appeals from state courts are also possible in unusual circumstances, e.g., *Thompson* v. *Louisville*, 362 U.S. 199 (1960).

usually presents what is called a 'petition for certiorari.'[1] In this document he seeks to demonstrate not so much that the decision below is wrong as that the issues involved are of national significance, warranting consideration and decision by the highest court of the land. Each petition is considered by all nine justices, who then vote whether to accept the case. If four of them vote to grant the petition for review, the case comes up and is heard on the merits[2] by substantially the same procedures that apply in any other American appellate court, The appellant furnishes a record of proceedings below, and then each side submits a written argument called a 'brief', stating the issues involved, the authorities relied on in the way of constitutional provisions, statutes, cases and other materials, and the reasons why the judgment below should be affirmed, reversed or modified. These are lengthy documents, sometimes running to 50 or more printed pages. Copies are exchanged between the parties and furnished to each member of the Court well before oral argument, so that they can be studied in advance. When the case is heard orally, arguments are limited to thirty minutes or one hour for each side.[3] The Court does not consider and decide cases one at a time, but hears oral arguments in batches of a dozen or more cases in a single week, then adjourns to consider its decisions and prepare written opinions. Decisions are not pronounced orally from the bench at the conclusion of argument, but customarily reserved until the judges have had ample time to discuss and formulate their views. They try to reach a unanimous conclusion and embody it in a single opinion, but when that is not possible (and often it is not), the judges prepare majority and dissenting or concurring opinions, sometimes all three in a single case.

Annually, about 3,000 petitions for certiorari are submitted

---

[1] The contents of the petition and the governing rules are found in Sup. Ct. R. 19–27.

[2] See dissents of Frankfurter, J., in *Rogers* v. *Missouri* Pac. R. Co., 352 U.S. 500 (1957); and *Dick* v. *New York Life Ins. Co.*, 359 U.S. 437 (1959).

[3] The procedural steps are outlined in Sup. Ct. R. 33–52.

to the Supreme Court. Only a small percentage are granted.[1] In addition, there are a small number of cases where appeals can be taken as of right. These are ones involving what might be loosely called a conflict of sovereignty—where a federal court has held a state statute unconstitutional, or where a state court has held a federal statute unconstitutional, or has upheld its own state statute against the claim that it violates the Federal Constitution.[2] Adding such cases to those where review is granted as a matter of discretion, the Supreme Court still hears relatively few cases and renders full opinions in only about 120 of them each year. About one third of these are criminal cases, the rest civil.[3]

The role of the Supreme Court and of the federal judicial system in general is often misunderstood. Warren E. Burger is symbolically the head of the entire American judiciary, but his title of 'Chief Justice of the United States' refers to his position in the federal hierarchy. He has no control over state courts except in the way I have just described—as one member of a court having ultimate appellate jurisdiction over some, but by no means all, state decisions. As for administrative control over the state courts, he has none. Neither does the Judicial Conference of the United States. It is a body created by Act of Congress to coordinate the activities of the federal courts and improve their operation, and it is composed of federal judges exclusively.[4] Neither does the Administrative Office of the United States Courts, which gathers statistics and performs housekeeping chores only for the federal courts.[5] Neither does the new Federal Judicial Center, which carries on research and coordinates educational programs for

---

[1] For an annual analysis of the business undertaken by the Supreme Court and a statistical summary of the disposition of the cases submitted to the court for appeal, see *Harvard Law Review*, annual November issue, and the *Annual Report of the Director of the Administrative Office of the United States Courts;* see also, opinion of Frankfurter, J., in *Maryland* v. *Baltimore Radio Show*, 338 U.S 912 (1950).

[2] 28 U.S.C. §§ 1254 and 1257.

[3] *Supra*, n. 1.

[4] 28 U.S.C. § 331.

[5] 28 U.S.C. §§ 601–608.

the federal judiciary only.[1] The various agencies I have mentioned constitute in combination the administrative machinery for the federal courts, but they do not serve the needs of the state courts.

Each state judicial system is complete in itself. It may or may not have administrative machinery comparable to that found in the federal system. Some states have unified court systems which are centrally administered, usually by the Chief Justice of the state with the assistance of an administrative office. It is his job to keep constantly aware of how judicial business all over the state is being processed, to transfer judges from courts which are not busy to those overburdened with work, and to inaugurate or at least suggest any improvements in procedure or administration that are needed from time to time to enable courts to dispose of their cases fairly and expeditiously. Other states have virtually no central administration—only a motley collection of fiercely independent courts, held together only by the thin threads of appellate review.[2]

The trend today is away from such chaos toward centralized court administration, but about 20 states still lack statewide administrative offices.[3]

Because of the dispersion of control over state and federal courts, responsibility for judicial administration is not concentrated in any one place in the United States, as it is—to a large extent at any rate—in the Lord Chancellor's office and the Home Office in England. It tends to become everybody's business— and possibly, some might add, 'therefore nobody's business.' In addition to official agencies in the various states and in the federal government, there are many private and quasi-governmental

---

[1] 28 U.S.C. §§ 620–629; see also, Clark, 'The New Federal Judicial Center', 54 A.B.A.J. 743 (1968).

[2] Litke, 'The Modernization of the Minor Courts', 50 J. Am. Jud. Soc. 67 (1966); Winters, 'The National Movement to Improve the Administration of Justice', 48 J. Am. Jud. Soc. 17 (1964).

[3] Tydings, 'A French Approach to Judicial Administration, 50 J. Am. Jud. Soc. 44 (1966); McWilliams, 'Court Integration and Unification in the Model Judicial Article', 47 J. Am. Jud. Soc. 13 (1963); Klein, 'Judicial Adminstration', 1967, Ann. Survey of Amer. L. 663.

agencies that are concerned with the subject. The Commissioners on Uniform State Laws draft and promote the passage in their respective states of identical statutes on such subjects as negotiable instruments[1] and the rules of evidence[2] and reciprocal statutes on such subjects as the interstate extradition of persons accused of crime[3] and the enforcing of support orders against husbands who desert their wives.[4] The National Conference of Chief Justices of the various states and the National Conference of State Court Administrators and the National Conference of Bar Presidents all meet once a year to provide forums for their respective members to discuss common problems and exchange information and ideas. The Appellate Judges Seminar at New York University, the National College of Trial Judges and the National College of Juvenile Court Judges provide educational programs for judges from all over the nation.[5] The American Judicature Society publishes a monthly journal covering new developments in judicial administration and providing comparative data on such matters as judicial salaries, tenure, retirement and removal. The Institute of Judicial Administration acts as a management consultant to such state and federal courts as wish to avail themselves of its service, and it carries on a broad scale program of research into all aspects of judicial administration from the construction of courthouses and the preparation of judicial budgets to the internal operating procedures of appellate courts. These are only a few of the many agencies working for improvements in the courts nationally and towards uniformity in the administration of justice in America. They supplement the other unifying forces which I discussed earlier.

I have been speaking so far only about the impact of federalism on American courts. There are other consequences of having a written constitution which are also important.

---

[1] Uniform Negotiable Instruments Act.
[2] Uniform Evidence Act.
[3] Uniform Extradition Act.
[4] Uniform Reciprocal Enforcement of Support Act.
[5] Karlen, 'Judicial Education', 52 A.B.A.J. 1049 (1966).

C

One of these is a more rigid separation of powers than is known in England. The United States Constitution and the constitutions of the various states attempt to isolate the judicial branch of government from the executive and legislative branches far more completely than in England. The United States has no such officer as the Lord Chancellor who, while heading the judicial establishment, also serves as a cabinet minister and presides over the House of Lords. Dealings between American courts and the other agencies of government are pretty much at arm's length. American courts have no representative in the inner councils of power to plead their case for additional manpower or higher budgets or better facilities. By the same token, however, they are not responsible to the legislative or the executive branch of government for failing to do their work or for doing it badly. Despite the popular election of many judges in the United States, and despite their relatively short terms of office, they are not nearly as accountable to the public as are English judges. Perhaps the whole judicial system of the United States is so complex and confusing, so Hydra-headed, that ordinary citizens do not even attempt to understand or control it.

Another profound effect of a written constitution is that Americans are not free to manage their judicial affairs in any way that seems fair, sensible and efficient. Instead they are limited by constitutional restrictions, both federal and state.

A surprising number of provisions in the Federal Constitution are directly concerned with the administration of justice. They cannot be changed except by the exceedingly cumbersome and difficult procedure of constitutional amendment.[1] For example, the Constitution provides that Supreme Court judges must be appointed by the President with the advice and consent of the Senate. If Congress became convinced that the appointing power should be elsewhere, or that the President's power should be restricted to candidates nominated by an impartial commission, or that the Senate's role should be curtailed or expanded, it

---

[1] U.S. Const. art. V; see also, *Dillon* v. *Gloss*, 256 U.S. 368 (1921).

would be powerless to act. Any legislation it might pass to put such ideas into effect would be struck down as unconstitutional by the Supreme Court. Similarly the Federal Constitution provides that no person shall be held to answer for a capital or other infamous crime except upon the accusation of a grand jury. If Congress thought the grand jury should be eliminated and its functions performed by magistrates conducting preliminary examinations, again it would be powerless to act.[1]

The two restrictions I have mentioned are among the provisions of the Constitution which apply only to the federal courts. There are other procedural regulations in the Constitution which apply only to state courts such as those defining the territorial limits for service of civil process[2] and the effect of civil judgments rendered by the courts of one state in other states.[3] There are still others, applying both to state and federal courts, which deal with such matters as bail, the right to trial by jury[4] and the right to counsel in criminal cases,[5] the privilege against self-incrimination,[6] and the admissibility in evidence of confessions[7] and illegally obtained evidence.[8]

These procedural rules in the Constitution have occupied much of the time and attention of the Supreme Court of the United States, which is the final arbiter of their meaning and application. The Court has interpreted them liberally and applied them broadly. For example, the provision that the accused is entitled to the 'Assistance of Counsel for his defence' was once understood

---

[1] I. B. Schwartz, *Commentary, supra*, p. 4, n. 2, at 17; *Supreme Court and Supreme Law* (E. Cann ed. 1954); C. L. Black, *The People and the Court*, Ch. IV (1960). A comprehensive survey of the origin and growth of judicial review is to be found in Haines, *American Doctrine of Judicial Supremacy*, generally, Chs. VIII and XV (2d ed. 1932); and *Marbury* v. *Madison*, 1 Cranch 137 (1803), the leading case.

[2] U.S. Const. amend. XIV § 1, as interpreted in *Pennoyer* v. *Neff*, 95 U.S. 714 (1877), and many cases following it.

[3] U.S. Const. art. IV, § 1.

[4] *Duncan* v. *Louisiana*, 88 S. Ct. 1444 (1968).

[5] *Gideon* v. *Wainwright*, 372 U.S. 335 (1963).

[6] *Griffin* v. *California*, 380 U.S. 609 (1965).

[7] *Miranda* v. *Arizona*, 384 U.S. 436 (1966).

[8] *Mapp* v. *Ohio*, 367 U.S. 643 (1961).

to be applicable only in the federal courts and to mean only that the accused had the right to have his own privately retained lawyer speak for him in court. The Supreme Court held, however, that it governed in the state courts as well, and that the language meant that if the accused was too poor to employ a lawyer, he had the right to be provided with legal representation at no cost to himself.[1] From this it can be seen that constitutional interpretation is less an exercise in semantics than an opportunity to determine profound questions of social policy.

One effect of such Supreme Court decisions is to standardize and make uniform some aspects of judicial administration throughout the nation, thus reinforcing the unifying forces I discussed earlier and counteracting to some extent the centrifugal force of federalism. Another effect is to restrict the freedom of state courts and state legislatures to experiment with new techniques of administering justice, even when they are convinced that such techniques would be swifter, more economical or more fair. They are further restricted by state constitutions, which largely duplicate but also supplement the restrictions imposed by the Federal Constitution. For example, although the federal right to trial by jury in civil cases has not been extended to state courts,[2] almost all state constitutions contain substantially similar guarantees. Hence if the people of a state wished to follow the example of England and dispense with civil juries they could do so only by amending their state constitution. This is not nearly as difficult an undertaking as amending the Federal Constitution, but it is not easy. Despite the fact that the United States has a far larger and politically more powerful legal profession than that of England, reform is much harder to achieve in the United States than in England. Partly that is because of the restrictions imposed by written constitutions; partly it is because responsibility for the administration of justice is not centralized in the United States the way it is in England; and partly it is because the American

---

[1] *Gideon* case, *supra*, p. 19, n. 5.

[2] *Walker* v. *Sauvinet*, 92 U.S. 90 (1875).

legal profession, unlike that in England, is not a close-knit group with common traditions and common goals.

I have been speaking so far only about the provisions in the federal and state constitutions which deal with judicial administration as such. The most important and prominent provisions, however, including the famous 'due process of law' and 'equal protection' clauses[1] deal with matters of general social and economic policy. They too have a profound effect upon American courts, for they plunge the courts into all sorts of problems which in England and many other countries are considered beyond the scope of judicial determination. Two landmark cases of the Supreme Court will make this clear. In *Brown* v. *Board of Education*,[2] the Supreme Court outlawed racial segregation in the public schools; and in *Baker* v. *Carr*[3] it held that voting districts had to be structured in such a way as to equalize the political strength of all voters—'one man, one vote'. The effect of such decisions is not only to involve the Supreme Court itself in problems of education and politics, but also to involve all the lower courts, state and federal, in the same problems, for those courts are required to apply and implement the Supreme Court decisions. Additional burdens of work are thus imposed on judicial machinery already overburdened in the processing of routine civil and criminal cases.

One final effect of deciding constitutional cases remains to be considered. That is a subtle alteration in the nature of the judicial process, at least at the appellate level. Constitutional provisions are not only hard to change, but also generally vague in their terms, consisting often of such concepts as 'due process of law'. This combination is a heady challenge to judges. Their job is not merely to interpret language such as that found in a contract or a statute. It is rather to give specific content to majestic generalities as applied to concrete situations and to constantly re-examine old solutions in the light of new problems and new attitudes toward

[1] U.S. Const. amend. XIV ,§ 1.
[2] 347 U.S. 483 (1954).
[3] 369 U.S. 186 (1962).

them. As Mr. Justice Brandeis remarked in a dissenting opinion in the Supreme Court of the United States:

> '*Stare decisis* is usually the wise policy, because in most matters it is more important that the applicable rule of law be settled than that it be settled right . . . . But in cases involving the Federal Constitution, where correction through legislative action is practically impossible, this Court has often overruled its earlier decisions. The Court bows to the lesson of experience and the force of better reasoning, recognizing that the process of trial and error, so fruitful in the physical sciences, is appropriate also in the Judicial function.'[1]

Constitutional interpretation, in other words, leads to an erosion of the traditional doctrine of *stare decisis*. Precedent becomes less important than current policy. For this reason, the Supreme Court can be more easily understood as a legislative body than as a judicial tribunal. Nowhere is this more clear than where the Supreme Court overrules a case prospectively. It sometimes says that the new rule it is announcing does not apply to the case before it, but only to future cases.[2]

If the relaxation of *stare decisis* stopped with constitutional cases in the Supreme Court, the consequences would not be too serious. But it does not stop there. The same approach has spread in the Supreme Court from constitutional issues to non-constitutional issues, such as the interpretation of statutes, and from the Supreme Court of the United States to other appellate courts, both federal and state, even when they are dealing with common law problems having no constitutional implications. They overrule prior decisions with what must appear to English

---

[1] *Burnet* v. *Coronado Oil & Gas Co.*, 285 U.S. 393, 406–408 (1932); see also, *Green* v. *U.S.*, 356 U.S. 165 (1958), Black, J., dissenting.

[2] *Great Northern Co.* v. *Sunburst Oil and Refining Co.*, 287 U.S. 358 (1932); see also, Schaefer, 'The Control of Sunbursts: Techniques of Prospective Overruling', 22 Record of the Assn. of the Bar of the City of N.Y. 394 (1967); Jackson, 'Decisional Law and Stare Decisis', 30 A.B.A.J. 334 (1944); Friedmann, 'Limits of Judicial Lawmaking and Prospective Overruling', 29 Mod. L. Rev. 593 (1966).

eyes reckless abandon.[1] Trial courts still feel constrained to abide by the precedents established by tribunals above them, but the appellate tribunals feel free to depart from their own precedents whenever they seem to have outlived their usefulness. They are determined, it seems, to correct old errors and to adapt the law to new conditions and changing attitudes. In short, American courts follow a far looser doctrine of precedent than that currently in vogue in England, even despite the announcement of the Lord Chancellor in 1966 that thenceforth the House of Lords would feel free to depart from a previous decision when the Law Lords deemed it proper and just to do so.[2] So far no drastic change in approach has materialized. English judges still believe that their main function is to apply the law, not to make or remake it.

SUMMARY

I should like to conclude by summarizing some of the differences between England and the United States which arise from their divergent histories and from the fact that the United States has a written constitution while England does not.

First, as against England's single unified system of courts, the United States has 51 different systems.

Second, because Americans take the theory of separation of powers more seriously than Englishmen, American courts are less accountable to the public than those of England.

Third, American courts and legislative bodies are less free than those of England to effectuate needed changes in judicial administration, being restricted by federal and state constitutional limitations.

[1] Schaefer, 'Precedent and Policy', 34 U. of Chi. L. Rev. 3 (1966); D. Karlen, *Appellate Courts in the United States and England* 66 (1963); Jackson, *Stare Decisis, supra*, p. 22, n. 2; see, e.g., *Nye* v. *U.S.*, 313 U.S. 33 (1941); *Durham* v. *U.S.*, 214 F. 2d 862 (D.C.Cir. 1954); *Chmielewski* v. *Marich*, 2 Ill. 2d 568, 119 N.E. 2d 247 (1954).

[2] [1966] 1 W.L.R. 1234 [Eng.—July 26, 1966]; see also, Leach, 'Revisionism in the House of Lords; the Bastion of Rigid Stare Decisis Falls', 80 Harv. L. Rev. 797 (1967); Birnbaum, 'Stare Decisis v. Judicial Activism', 54 A.B.A.J. 482 1968).

Fourth, American courts are involved in social, political and economic problems to a greater extent than those of England.

Finally, the American doctrine of precedent is far less rigid than that followed in England.

These, however, are not the only differences. In the next two Chapters I shall discuss other differences of equal importance.

Chapter 2   *Personnel of the Law*

'For forms of government let fools contest,
Whate'er is best administered is best.'

Alexander Pope

The quality of justice depends ultimately upon the people who administer it. After discussing the judges, I shall turn to other people who also have important roles to play.

SELECTION OF JUDGES

One of the most striking characteristics of American judges is that almost to a man they are creatures of politics. Most state judges are chosen by popular election, just like governors, mayors or legislators. They run for office against other candidates and in some places on party tickets. They make speeches, kiss babies, go to church dinners, plaster their pictures on billboards and proclaim their virtues from cruising sound trucks. All this is done in the name of Jacksonian democracy so that judges, like other public officials, will be responsive to the will of the people. But what can ordinary citizens know about the qualities needed in a judge? How can they make an intelligent choice? And what kind of issues can be put forward in a political campaign for a judgeship? Are Republican judges different from Democratic judges? Can one candidate promise that he will enforce the law, and his opponent that he will not enforce it—legitimately, that is? Or can one candidate promise that he will decide cases in favor of plaintiffs, and the other that he will decide in favor of defendants?

Popular election of judges is a farce, and a hoax on the public. At least this is true in metropolitan areas, and probably is true everywhere. Most citizens seem to sense this subconsciously, and act accordingly. Their apathy is demonstrated by their failure to even try to find out anything about the men running for judicial office, and by the fact that hardly any of them can say the day after the election which judicial candidates received their own votes. This has been demonstrated by polls.[1] What happens is that most people simply vote the party line when it comes to judges. The result is that the real choice of judges is left in the hands of the political leaders who nominate them. The choice almost inevitably falls upon the party faithful—those who have performed political chores like 'getting out the vote', raising money and managing campaigns. These party workers may or may not be competent lawyers who have the potential of becoming competent judges, but that is incidental. The main thrust is to keep the party going by rewarding the faithful. The entire process is almost invisible, for it is next to impossible for the public to see how or why judicial selections are made, or by whom. This is not to suggest that a man should be disqualified from judicial office because he has been politically active. Quite the contrary. That experience may make him a better judge, especially when he is called upon to deal with questions of social policy. The point is that politics should not predominate in the selection of judges to the extent of overshadowing professional competence and qualities of character.

The elective system is qualified in one important practical way: when a vacancy occurs prior to the expiration of a judge's normal term of office (as when he dies or retires), it is filled temporarily by executive appointment. The new judge may then

---

[1] E. Roper, *A Study of Voter Awareness of Certain Candidates for Office in New York States*. (Prepared for the Citizens Union Research Foundation 1954 and 1966); League of Women Voters, Survey Poll on Voters' Knowledge Regarding Judicial Candidates. (1964) (on file, Library of Institute of Judicial Administration).

run in the next election with a better than average expectation of being elected for a full term. In other words, even in an elective system, many judges come to office originally by appointment.[1] A more visible selection process is the appointive method, used in the federal courts and the courts of some states. The chief executive —President or Governor, as the case may be—appoints the judges subject to confirmation by a legislative body, national or state.[2] Here responsibility for judicial selection is concentrated on the chief executive who, at least theoretically, can be held accountable at the bar of public opinion for any mistakes he makes. Conceivably, although I have never known this to happen, the chief executive might himself be denied re-election because of the poor quality of his judicial appointments. More likely, however, they will be forgotten in the welter of more exciting issues. The process of appointment is not necessarily any less political than the process of popular election. Chief executives are not always sensitive to judicial talent, but they are sensitive to political talent, and almost inevitably they have political debts which can be discharged by appointments to judicial office. Politics also enters into the legislative process of confirming executive appointments to the judiciary, as was recently demonstrated in dramatic fashion when the Senate refused to confirm President Nixon's appointment of Clement Haynsworth (Chief Judge of the U.S. Court of Appeals for the Fourth Circuit) to the Supreme Court of the United States.

No one who has watched closely how judicial appointments are made in the United States can pretend that the appointive process is non-political. Yet the general impression is that appointed judges, by and large, are superior to elected judges. If that impression is correct, it is not because politics is absent from the appointive process, but partly because many lawyers who would refuse to subject themselves to the indignity of popular election are willing to accept appointment—even to seek

[1] *American Judicature Society Report on Judicial Selection and Tenure* (Feb. 1967), p. 5.

[2] E.g., U.S. Const. art. II § 2; N. J. Const. art. VI, § 6, par. 1.

it actively through politically powerful friends—and partly because responsibility for judicial selection is more concentrated and more visible.

The evils of both popular elections and executive appointments are compounded by short tenure. In some states, judges serve for terms of only two, four or six years.[1] Unless they are beneficiaries of a local tradition of re-electing sitting judges almost automatically, they may have to curry political favor even after they are on the bench, and periodically go through the process of either re-appointment or popular re-election.

In an effort to cure some of the deficiencies and retain some of the virtues of both the elective and appointive methods of selecting judges, a third method has been devised. It is most commonly called the 'Missouri plan', because that is the state which first adopted it, but it is also known by many other names, including the 'American Judicature plan', because that Society devised it, the 'American Bar Association plan', because that group endorsed it, and 'The Merit plan', because it is supposed to eliminate politics from judicial selection.[2] Many variations of the plan are possible, but in essence it works this way: a non-partisan or at least bi-partisan nominating commission is established; it looks over the field of judicial candidates and nominates for each vacancy three to five persons it considers qualified; their names are submitted to the chief executive who then makes his final choice from the names submitted. The judge is appointed for a limited time—say two years, and then if he wishes to continue in office, he must submit his name to the electorate. He does not run against any other candidate or on any party ticket, but simply on his record, and the sole question to be answered by the voters is whether the judge should be retained in office.

The Missouri plan has some value in making the process of

[1] XVII Book of the States 108 (1968).

[2] Mo. Const. art. V, § 29(a), (b), (c); see also, Rosenman, 'A Better Way to Select Judges,' 48 J. Am. Jud. Soc. 86 (1964); 'Twenty-Five Years under the Missouri Plan', 49 J. Am. Jud. Soc. 81 (1965); see also, Hemker, 'Experience under the Missouri Non-Partisan Court Plan', 43 J. Am. Jud. Soc. 159 (1960).

judicial selection more visible and in screening out candidates who are clearly unfit for judicial office, but it is very questionable whether it accomplishes all its advocates claim. Politics is not necessarily eliminated. It may merely be transferred from political clubs to bar associations. Furthermore, the selection process can be manipulated. For example, the governor or mayor, having the power of final selection may be able to 'pack' the nominating commission by naming some or all of its members, or he may himself or through his political associates submit to the commission the name of his own candidate; and if that person survives the screening, choose him rather than any of the other candidates approved by the commission. In short, all that may be accomplished is a deception of the public.[1] Furthermore, the Missouri plan preserves the illusion of popular election of judges without giving the people any real say in the matter. If they are incapable of determining who should be chosen as judges initially, it would seem that they must be equally incapable of appraising the judicial records of those who are chosen and determining which of them should be retained in office. The main effect of the Missouri plan may be to give judges life tenure without a frank disclosure of that fact to the public.

Perhaps that is why the Missouri plan, although it has now been vigorously advocated for over 60 years, has not swept the country as its supporters think it should. People may prefer the more forthright even if more ruggedly political methods of straight appointment and popular election. Innocuous as the Missouri plan is, it is in effect only in 15 states by the most generous count,[2] and in most of those, only for a few courts. There is no empirical proof that the Missouri plan produces better judges than the elective or straight appointive plans.[3]

[1] E. Costikyan, *Behind Closed Doors*, Ch. 17 (1966); see also, Review of Costikyan's book, Karlen, New York Law Journal, Aug. 12, 1966, p. 4, cols. 4 and 5.
[2] American Judicature Society, Report No. 18, '*The Extent of Adoption of the Non-Partisan Appointive-Elective Plan for the Selection of Judges* (1969).
[3] Opinion evidence of lawyers in Missouri is to the effect that 'better' judges are produced by the Missouri plan than by an elective system. Watson and Downing, *The Politics of the Bench and Bar* 345 (1969).

In view of the widespread dissatisfaction that exists in the legal profession and the public with the present methods of selecting judges, and the endless debate over the merits and demerits of the three methods I have described, it is curious that no one has seriously urged that we might do well to copy the English method and vest the power to select judges in an officer directly responsible for the operation of the judicial system. In the State of New York, for example, it would be possible by constitutional amendment to vest the power of selection in the chief judge of the Court of Appeals. He is the administrative head not only of his own court but also of the entire state judicial system. Through the Judicial Conference and its administrative board, he has an intelligence network which rivals that of the English Lord Chancellor for knowing what is happening in courts all over the state and for learning from other judges which lawyers are likely prospects for elevation to the bench. Knowing intimately the nature of judicial work, he would know what qualities to look for in a judge, and he would have a personal stake in the selection process, because the functioning of the system for which he was responsible would depend upon the quality of the judges he chose. His own reputation would depend in large part on how well he performed the task of judicial selection. This would counteract, perhaps overcome completely, the effect of the chief judge himself being a product of political choice. At least there is reason to hope so, based upon the way the Lord Chancellor's office operates.

The idea of having the chief judge of a state select other judges is not as impractical as it might first appear. In all jurisdictions, except the few where judges enjoy life tenure, the chief judge is periodically accountable either to the people or the chief executive. He may be directly elected or appointed to his post for a limited term of years, or, as is more common, he may become a member of the state supreme court by election or appointment and then become chief judge by seniority or by vote of his colleagues. Even so, when his term expires, his record is open to scrutiny. If he had the power to select judges, his judicial appointments would be an important part of that record. The task would not be unduly burdensome, because in most states the number of judicial vacancies is small. Even in New York or California, the number is small compared to the number of vacancies which have to be filled by the Lord Chancellor. He, while carrying on his manifold other duties, selects all of the magistrates as well as all of the regular judges—a far greater number of officials than the number of professional judges found in any American jurisdiction.

Perhaps we have made, almost unconsciously, a start in the direction of having judges select judges. In a few jurisdictions in the United States, judicial officers at the lowest level are chosen by judges at the level immediately above them. Thus in the federal system, district judges choose referees in bankruptcy and federal magistrates.[1] Both of these sets of officials exercise specialised jurisdiction under close control. In Illinois and Virginia, much the same pattern exists—trial judges select subordinate magistrates.[2] Furthermore, in places where Missouri type judicial screening panels are in operation, judges are frequently included in their membership. The model judicial article, prepared and advocated by the American Bar Association for state constitutions, generally adopts the Missouri plan of judicial selection, but it also provides that if the chief executive fails to appoint a judge from the list of judicial nominees submitted to him within a specified period of time after the list reaches him, his power to make the appointment passes to the chief judge of the state[3]. In view of these precedents in our own country, it seems strange that it has occurred to no one that the idea might be extended to judges at all levels.

Despite the harsh things I have said about American methods of selecting judges, I would not like to leave the impression that

---

[1] 11 U.S.C. § 62; Pub. L. 90–578, Oct. 17, 1968, 82 Stat. 1107, 28 U.S.C.A. 604, 631–639.

[2] Ill. Const. art. VI § 12; Code of Va., Title 16, § 16.1–16.7. See also, Kingdon, 'Trial Justice System in Virginia', 23 J. Am. Jud. Soc. 216 (1940); Institute of Judicial Administration (hereinafter abbreviated I.J.A.), *The Justice of the Peace Today* 4–13 (1965).

[3] A.B.A. Judicial Administration Section, *Model Judicial Article* (1962).

there are no good American judges. There are many judges who are thoroughly competent and conscientious, and some who qualify to be described as great judges by any standard, in any league. This is not because of American methods of selection, but in spite of them. Competent men who want to become judges in the United States learn to play the game of judicial selection as it is played, whether they like it or not. They master the art of politics as they master other skills.

THE SIZE OF THE JUDICIARY

Another remarkable thing about American judges is that there are so many of them. In New York City alone, there are more full time professional judges than in all of England—367 judges for a population of about eight million,[1] compared to England's 286 full time professionals for a population of about 50 million.[2] Moreover, new judges are constantly being added. In 1968, for example, 85 new judgeships were created in New York City.[3] In 1966 Congress created 35 new federal judgeships, and in 1968, 16 more.[4] Still more are being asked and may well be created soon.

Part of the explanation of England's having relatively few judges (although not all of the explanation), lies in its system of magistrates, who dispose of about 97 per cent of all the criminal cases in England[5] as well as a substantial amount of matrimonial litigation.[6] There are justices of the peace in the United States also, but they are relatively few in number and usually found only in rural areas. In some states they have disappeared completely, and in places where they still exist, they are almost as different from English justices as night is from day. They have the same name, they also serve part time, and they also need not be legally

[1] *Thirteenth Annual Report of the Judicial Conference of the State of New York* (1968), pp. 318, A–48, A–49.
[2] R. M. Jackson, *The Machinery of Justice in England* 28 (5th ed. 1967).
[3] New York Law Journal, Vol. 159, No. 102, p. 1, cols. 7, 8, May 24, 1968.
[4] 28 U.S.C. § 133.
[5] Jackson, *supra*, n. 2, at 122.
[6] Jackson, *supra*, n. 2, at 201.

trained, but there the similarity stops. American justices are compensated—in some places by fees, in others by salaries; but the salaries are so small as to attract few competent and dedicated people. In most states, they are chosen by popular election and too often their only qualification is faithful political service. They enjoy little prestige—instead mostly ridicule and contempt, sometimes good natured, sometimes not. Their ranks are not leavened, as in England, by the presence of professional judges working part time and without pay as magistrates. They do not sit in panels, but individually, and they do not have the assistance of legally trained clerks. Finally, their jurisdiction to 'hear and determine' is limited to trivial cases, civil and criminal. Traffic offenses and bill collections account for the great bulk of their work.[1]

JURIES

Because so much of the work that is done by magistrates in England is done by full time professional judges in the United States, something in the way of public understanding and acceptance of the law has been lost. We compensate for this to a degree by using juries more extensively than England does. Juries in civil cases as well as criminal are the main vehicles in the United States for citizen involvement in the work of the courts.

This is not entirely a matter of deliberate choice, for state and federal constitutions require juries in certain types of cases.[2] In the federal courts and in some state court systems, grand juries are constitutionally required to indict persons accused of serious crimes.[3] In other state systems grand juries have been eliminated by state constitutional provisions on the ground that they only

---

[1] I.J.A., *The Justice of the Peace Today*, Table I & II (1965); see also, Karlen, *Anglo-American Criminal Justice* 57–60 (1967)

[2] U.S. Const. art. II § 2, Amend. VI, Amend. VII; see, e.g., Wis. Const. art. I §§ 5, 6; Alaska Const. art. I, §§ 11, 16; and *Duncan* v. *Louisiana*, 88 S. Ct. 1444 (1968).

[3] U.S. Const. Amend. V; see e.g. Alaska Const. art. I. § 8; N. J. Const. art. I, par. 8.

D

duplicate the work done by magistrates or judges in preliminary hearings.[1] Petit juries, on the other hand, are guaranteed by both state and federal constitutions for the trial of all serious crimes and for civil actions 'at common law.'[2] The right to trial by jury is not extended to all cases, but preserved only in cases where it had previously existed.[3] This eliminates prosecutions for petty crimes,[4] and certain civil actions, including those formerly tried in courts of equity.[5] Even so limited, however, the right to trial by jury is far more extensive in the United States than in England. Whereas England tries virtually no civil cases by jury, we try a great many by jury, including claims for personal injury or wrongful death arising out of auto accidents.[6] Whereas England tries by jury only 2 or 3 per cent of its criminal cases—those which reach the Assizes or Quarter Sessions Courts—we try by jury all but the smallest criminal cases—those which can be disposed of at the magistrate level.[7]

The right to trial by jury in the United States is defended not so much on the ground that it induces citizen participation in the administration of justice, as upon the ground that it provides better protection for the rights of litigants. This is a measure of American distrust of judges, a distrust which arises from our methods of selecting them and from the malfunctioning of our judicial system, and which has been documented by public opinion polls. It also goes far toward explaining why jury service does not achieve the kind of citizen participation that the

[1] See e.g., Ill. Const. art. I, § 8, Mich. Const. art. I. See also, Karlen, *Anglo-American Criminal Justice*, *supra*, p. 33, n. 1, at 149–153; California Grand Jury System, 8 Stan. L. Rev. 631 (1956).

[2] U.S. Const. art. III § 2; U.S. Const. Amend. VI, VII; see e.g., Conn. Const. art. I, § 19; N.Y. Const. art. I, § 2.

[3] James, *Civil Procedure* 337 *et seq.* (1965).

[4] See e.g., *Duncan* v. *Louisiana, supra*, p. 33, n. 2, *District of Columbia* v. *Clawans*, 300 U.S. 617 (1937).

[5] James, *supra*, n. 3, at 372–377.

[6] Jackson, *supra*, p.32, n. 2, at 72–73, 315–317; Karlen, 'Can a State Abolish the Civil Jury?' 1965 Wis. L. Rev. 102.

[7] Jackson, *supra*, p. 32, n. 2, at 112–113, 317–318; Karlen, *Anglo-American Criminal Justice, supra* p. 33, n. 1, at 179.

magistrate system in England achieves. Jurors are treated like conscripts, who must serve whether they wish to or not. They are chosen mostly by lot, summoned peremptorily to court and then kept waiting around unconscionably while other cases are being tried and settled. They are questioned closely as to their fitness to serve and, as often as not, rejected. When, if at all, they are finally accorded the privilege of hearing a case, they are treated as if they were barely in possession of their faculties. They are prevented by the rules of evidence from hearing much relevant proof on the theory that they are incapable of properly weighing its probative value. They are warned against discussing the case between themselves until the judge directs them to retire for their deliberations.[1] They are sometimes prohibited from engaging in such normal activities as reading newspapers and watching television while the case is in progress, and occasionally even locked up to make sure they observe this prohibition.[2] They are excluded from whispered colloquies between the judge and the lawyers at the bench. They are instructed in the law, but in language they are not likely to understand because it is usually copied from appellate court opinions and directed not so much at the jurors as at the judges who may later review the case on appeal.[3] In most jurisdictions, they are given little or no help from the judge in understanding the facts because the judge is prohibited from commenting on or even summarising the evidence,[4] but they are subjected to plenty of partisan eloquence on that subject from the opposing lawyers. If the evidence is so one-sided that the judge concludes that reasonable men can reach only one result, the case is taken away from the jurors completely by a directed verdict on the theory that they cannot be trusted to act

[1] E.g., Handbook for Jurors in the Federal Courts, 26 F.R.D. 549, 556 (1960).

[2] A.B.A. Project on Minimum Standards for Criminal Justice, *Standards Relating to Fair Trial and Free Press*, Standard No. 3.5 (1966).

[3] See e.g., *Skidmore* v. *Baltimore & O. R. Co.*, 167 F. 2d 54 (2nd Cir. 1948).

[4] *Fifth Annual Report of the Judicial Council of New York*, 187–194 (1939); A.B.A. Project on Minimum Standards for Criminal Justice, *Standards Relating to Trial by Jury*, discussion following Standard No. 4.7 (1968).

like reasonable men.[1] When the jurors are allowed to decide a case, the judge may order a new trial if he thinks the verdict is wrong.[2]

In recent years, there has been a growing realization that jurors are not treated properly, but this pertains mainly to their creature comforts and the use made of their time. Even where efforts have been made to deal with these problems, the role of jurors is vastly different from the role of English magistrates, and not well calculated to lead to widespread public understanding and acceptance of the law.

THE LEGAL PROFESSION

The proper functioning of the courts depends not only upon judges and jurors, but also upon the legal profession. This is especially true where the adversary system of litigation is followed, as it is in both our nations.

The American legal profession is about fourteen times the size of England's, counting both barristers and solicitors. On a per capita basis, it is still more than three times the size of England's.[3] As might be expected from its size, our profession is not as homogeneous as England's. It is not centred in any one place, the way England's is in London, but fragmented among hundreds of cities in the 50 states and further fragmented by deep ideological differences. We do not speak with a single voice or all pull together in the same direction. Instead there is much tugging and hauling in opposite directions. That is one reason why legal reforms are harder to achieve in the United States than in England.

There are many other contrasts between the English legal profession and ours. The most obvious is that England's is divided into barristers and solicitors, while we have only one

[1] Fed. R.C.P. 50 (a); see also, *Neely* v. *Eby Construction Co., Inc.*, 386 U.S. 317 (1967); *Galloway* v. *U.S.*, 319 U.S. 372 (1943).

[2] Fed. R.C. P. 50 (b), (c), (d); R. 59; see also, *Montgomery Ward & Co.* v *Duncan*, 311 U.S. 243 (1940).

[3] American Bar Foundation, *The 1967 Lawyer Statistical Report* 12 (1968); Karlen, *Anglo-American Criminal Justice*, *supra*, p. 33, n. 1, at 30.

class of lawyers, authorized to do any kind of legal work, in court or out. Much could be said about this difference in terms of efficiency and the cost to litigants, but the distinction is so well known and the comparative merits of the two systems have been so thoroughly debated that I shall pass on to other distinctions between the two professions that are less well known.

SPECIALIZATION

One is the fact that American lawyers specialize more than English lawyers do in criminal cases. We use professional judges where England uses magistrates, and some of our professionals handle only criminal cases. We also use specialists to represent the prosecution and the defense.

Prosecution is in the hands of government officials who are usually elected and called 'district attorneys' and their subordinates whom they appoint. In urban areas, these men ordinarily serve full time and do no other work than prosecuting.[1] They do not represent defendants in criminal cases, nor do they handle civil cases for either side. In rural areas, they may serve part time and be allowed to carry on a private practice on the side, but they are not permitted to handle criminal cases for the defense; and they prosecute all criminal cases in their areas. The consequence is that the vast majority of lawyers in any American community, unlike those in England, are excluded from the work of prosecution. Thus in Manhattan, the heart of New York City, where there are about 30,000 lawyers,[2] the work of prosecution is concentrated in the hands of 102 lawyers who comprise the staff of the District Attorney and a few lawyers who comprise the criminal staff of his federal counterpart, the U.S. Attorney.[3]

Another consequence of having district attorneys is that

---

[1] Karlen, *Anglo-American Criminal Justice*, *supra*, p. 33, n. 1, at 24–29.

[2] American Bar Foundation, *Statistical Report*, *supra*, p. 36, n. 3, at 68.

[3] Mayer, '*Hogan's Office Is a Kind of Ministry of Justice*', N.Y. Times Magazine, July 23, 1967; U.S. Dept. of Justice, *Annual Report of the U.S. Attorney. Southern District of New York* 4 (1967).

politics can, and sometimes does, distort the function of prosecution. As creatures of politics themselves, district attorneys are subject to the temptation of using their powers more vigorously against leaders of the opposition party than against leaders of their own party. They are also subject to the temptation of compiling a strong record of convictions in order to further their own political futures. The office of district attorney is too often regarded as a stepping stone to a judgeship or other high political office.

The work of defense tends to be almost as specialized as the work of prosecution. Private lawyers who represent defendants able to pay legal fees are few in number, partly because there are few such defendants, and partly because many lawyers still look upon criminal defense work as somehow tainted and beneath their dignity.[1] The vast majority of defendants are indigent, and it is their representation that accounts for the bulk of defense work. At one time, the volume of indigent work was small because there was thought to be no need to provide free counsel except in the most serious cases, such as those in which the death penalty might be imposed. Judges assigned such work as there was fairly broadly among the lawyers in the community in order to equalize the burdens of providing free legal aid. In recent years, however, the volume of indigent work has increased very sharply. A growing social conscience in the profession and the public at large is reflected in a series of decisions by the Supreme Court of the United States holding that any indigent charged with a crime of even medium seriousness has a constitutional right to be represented by counsel at all stages of the proceeding without cost to himself[2]. The increased volume of indigent work has led to different methods of handling it, which in some places are replacing the more traditional method of judges assigning counsel *ad hoc*. These newly popularized methods are similar in

[1] See e.g., L. Silverstein, *Defense of the Poor in Criminal Cases in American State Courts—A Preliminary Survey* 6–13 (1964); Toll and Allison, 'Advocates for the Poor', 52 Judicature 321 (1969).

[2] *Gideon* v. *Wainwright*, 372 U.S. 335 (1963).

purpose to the English legal aid scheme, but markedly different in operation and effect. One of them is the establishment of a 'public defender' office at public expense—a defense counterpart to the district attorney's office.[1] Lawyers are employed in it full time to do nothing but represent indigent defendants in criminal cases. In communities where such offices exist, they do the lion's share of all defense criminal work to the virtual exclusion of the rest of the legal profession. Being specialists in criminal law, they may do a better job than would private general practitioners, but there is always a danger that their representation of clients may become over-institutionalized, impersonal, lacking in vigor, and perfunctory. In communities which do not have public defender offices, an alternative method of providing legal representation for indigents is sometimes found in the form of a legal aid society. Such an organization operates very much like a public defender office: its lawyers are employed full time to do substantially all of the indigent defense work for the community. It differs from a public defender office mainly in that it is a private, non-governmental organization, supported wholly or in part by private, voluntary contributions.[2]

One result of the methods I have just described is that in some communities most lawyers are spectators rather than participants in the process of administering criminal justice. Like members of the lay public, they merely look on while specialists do the work. It is not surprising that many of them lack understanding and refuse responsibility. The most they are likely to do is work for reforms in criminal justice, a matter about which I shall write later.

Happily, the old practice of assigning counsel for indigents from the whole legal profession has not died out. In some communities, it is still the dominant method of providing

[1] Decker, 'Report on the National Defender Program', Proceedings of the 17th Annual Meeting of the Conference of Chief Judges 51 (1964).

[2] Karlen, 'Legal Aid for the Criminal Accused in England and the United States: A Comparative Study', 63 Legal Aid Rev. 26 (1965); see also, Legal Aid Association, *Obtaining Justice for the Indigent Defendant Accused of Crime* 11 (1957).

legal aid. Increasingly, however, because of the mounting volume of indigent work, public funds are being made available to compensate lawyers for their services,[1] and more and more lawyers are becoming involved. Criminal practice is becoming more respectable than it used to be and good lawyers are beginning to drive bad lawyers out of the criminal courts. A larger segment of the legal profession is coming to understand criminal justice and be concerned with its quality. In the long run this may be as important to society as a whole as it is immediately helpful to the men on trial.

In civil matters, specialization is less common than in criminal matters. Nevertheless, it exists. Within large law firms in metropolitan areas, some lawyers do nothing but trust work, others nothing but corporate work, others nothing but litigation and so forth. Outside of such firms, there are also specialists in such fields as admiralty, patents and negligence.

So far as indigent clients are concerned, specialization also prevails—at least in large metropolitan communities like New York, where much of the poverty of the nation is concentrated. In such communities, the problems of the poor are increasingly being channelled into legal aid societies and neighbourhood law offices, in which lawyers are employed to devote their full time to advising and representing indigents. The profession as a whole in such communities does not get involved in the legal problems of the poor, except in the remote *pro bono publico* sense of assisting in the establishment of institutional methods for dealing with their problems.[2] One countervailing force is the practice by which some lawyers take certain cases—notably personal injury and wrongful death claims—on a contingent fee basis.[3] The lawyer

[1] See e.g., National Legal Aid and Defender Assoc., 1967 Summary of Proceedings of the 45th Annual Conference 278–300 (1967).

[2] Kirgis, 'Law Firms Could Better Serve the Poor', 55 A.B.A.J. 1232 (1969); Brennan, 'The Responsibility of the Legal Profession', 54 A.B.A.J. 121 (1968); see also. Pye and Garraty, 'The Involvement of the Bar in the War Against Poverty', 41 Notre Dame Lawyer 860 (1966); Bamberger, 'The Legal Services Program of the O.E.O.'. 41 Notre Dame Lawyer 847 (1966).

[3] I.J.A., *Contingent Fees in Personal Injury and Wrongful Death Actions in the United States* (1957).

gets no fee if he loses, but if he wins, he receives a percentage of the recovery, often as much as one third. This arrangement, whatever it may entail in the way of ambulance chasing, faked claims, exorbitant charges and unethical practices, makes available to some poor people in some types of cases a non-institutionalized form of legal representation. The same result might be accomplished in a more straightforward manner and without the accompanying evils if the United States were to adopt the English system of administering legal aid through the legal profession as a whole.[1]

LEGAL TRAINING

Those who aspire to become lawyers in the United States almost always receive their professional training in universities. Apprenticeship in a law office is still theoretically possible as an avenue leading to practice, but as a practical matter, it has died out during the present century because it has been unable to compete with the superior training offered by university law schools. Where it survives at all, it is not as a substitute for law school, but as a supplement.

A man ordinarily reaches law school at the age of about 22 after having spent four years in college and earned a B.A. degree. Then he spends three more years of full time study in law school, ending up at the age of about 25 with an LL.B. or J.D. degree, (These are exact equivalents, merely having different names in different schools.) Only then is he eligible to seek admission to what we call 'the bar', meaning the entire legal profession of a particular state.

One is not admitted to practice in the United States as a whole, but in a particular state, and then only in the state courts there. If he wishes to practice in the federal courts of his home state, he must go through an additional admission procedure, but this normally involves nothing more than the submission of

---

[1] R. Stevens and B. Abel-Smith, *Lawyers and the Courts: A Sociological Study of the English Legal Aid System* 1950–1965, Ch. 12 (1967); see also, Karlen, 'Legal Aid', *supra*, p. 39, n. 2, at 26 (1965).

papers proving his admission to practice in the state courts, and tends to be only a formality. If he wishes to practice in the courts of another state except on an *ad hoc* one-case basis, admission is more than a formality. It may even involve not only going through the same motions that a man fresh out of law school must follow, but also residence requirements that are almost impossible to satisfy. This is one of the consequences of having a federal type of government with 51 judicial systems instead of one.

Admission requirements vary from state to state, being promulgated by the Supreme Court of each state. Ordinarily they consist of the candidate having to pass a bar examination and satisfy a 'character committee' that he is morally fit to practice law. A bar examination is more comprehensive in scope than a law school examination in an individual course, but otherwise it is much the same type of test, with its content likely to be patterned after the law school curriculum. Sometimes the questions are even drafted by law school professors, but sometimes they are more picayune, dealing with small points of local practice which do little more than tax the memories of those who have to answer them. By and large, however, bar examinations are neither more nor less difficult than law school examinations. Their purpose is not so much to provide an independent appraisal of a candidate's legal ability by the practicing members of the profession as to see whether the candidate has really absorbed the training offered to him in law school. Thus we return again to the central importance of law schools in the training of lawyers and the relative unimportance in this regard of the practicing profession.

AMERICAN LAW SCHOOLS

American law schools are not remote from the life of the law, but very much part of it. Many of their teachers have practiced law for at least a few years either as private practitioners or as government attorneys. They tend to regard themselves primarily as lawyers, only secondarily as professors.

They are active in bar association activities and in law reform. They are paid good salaries, higher than those paid most other university professors and higher than those paid many judges. They teach practice as well as theory. For example, civil procedure and evidence are staples in the curriculum of every law school. Legal history and philosophy are not neglected, but they receive relatively little time. It is almost impossible today to find the forms of action being taught, and equity has disappeared as a separate course in favor of the fragmentation of its subject matter into other substantive and procedural courses. The law schools grapple with current problems, sometimes before they are recognized in the profession at large. Thus today we see courses and seminars in such areas as urban affairs, public housing, welfare law, and even the rights of students in university affairs. Many students find such courses more 'relevant' (to use their own language) than traditional subjects like contracts, torts and property.[1]

The teaching of law, unfortunately, is pretty much confined to law schools, where it is directed toward the vocational training of the relatively few people who want to become lawyers. As a subject of liberal education, law receives very little attention. In our undergraduate colleges, for example, we have no such program as exists in England, leading to a B.A. degree for those who do not want to become lawyers and yet want to understand law as an important part of their society and culture. In political science courses, much time is devoted to the executive and legislative branches of government, but precious little to the judicial branch. There are courses here and there on business law, constitutional law and similar specialties, and even a few courses of a more general nature, but these do not reach a large segment of the total population of our colleges and universities.[2]

---

[1] Ares, 'Legal Education and the Problems of the Poor', 17 J. of Legal Education 307 (1964).

[2] See e.g., H. Berman, *On the Teaching of Law in the Liberal Arts Curriculum* (1956); *Report of the Conference on Prelegal Education*, 6 J. of Legal Education 340 (1954).

Below the college level, law fares still worse as a subject of general education. Scant attention is paid to it even in courses where one might expect it to be treated. In courses on civics and social studies, for example, the emphasis is on current events, not upon the knowledge needed to understand those events. Students often graduate from high school without any conception of the difference between liberty and license, of the responsibilities which go along with rights, of the limits of dissent, of the methods by which peaceful change can be accomplished, or even of the rights of the majority. In short, too often high school graduates— or high school dropouts—do not understand what government is all about. This may be one cause—among many—of the increasing lawlessness of our young people, of their tendency to defy authority, of their impatience to see what they call 'social justice' done immediately. At least this is the view of some leaders of the American Bar Association, who are now attempting to launch a large-scale program of education in citizenship and law in the schools and colleges of the United States.[1]

The American failure to consider law as part of a general education contributes to the specialization I described and deplored earlier. By treating law as a concern only of specialists, we forfeit public understanding and support. Although we understand that war is too important to be entrusted to generals and that education is too important to be entrusted to teachers, we have not yet come to the realization that law is too important to be entrusted to lawyers.

CAREERS OF LAW GRADUATES

When a man graduates from law school, his ambition is not likely to be limited to becoming a draftsman of wills and contracts, or an advocate, or even a judge. He sees such goals as within his reach, but also other goals which may strike him as more exciting and more useful to society. He fancies himself a

[1] See e.g., *Coordinator and Public Relations Bulletin*, A.B.A. vol. 16, no. 1, p. 1. A Special Committee of the American Bar Association on Crime Prevention and Control is prominant in this effort.

social engineer, equipped to tackle almost any problem of society. Often he has an exaggerated notion of his ability and worth, but sometimes not. A surprising number of American law graduates become executives of corporations, government officials and leaders in all walks of life.[1]

One of the most sought-after jobs for the new law graduate is work for a judge as a 'law clerk'. Today most appellate judges and many trial judges as well are furnished at public expense with 'law clerks' to help them with research and the drafting of opinions. The law clerks are paid reasonable salaries and usually find their work interesting and highly educational. After serving for a year or two they go on to other jobs—practice or teaching or government service.

Those who stay with the law find not just one or two paths open to them, but many paths crisscrossing and intersecting. One who becomes an office lawyer, doing corporate work or conveyancing or the like, does not thereby forfeit the chance of becoming a judge. One who becomes a professor does not necessarily stay one all his life. He may later become a practitioner, or a court administrator, or a district attorney, or a judge. Some of our distinguished judges have come from academic life— Holmes, Rutledge, Frankfurter, Douglas, to mention a few who have been on the Supreme Court of the United States, and Schaefer of Illinois and Traynor of California, to mention a couple who have distinguished themselves on state courts. Even becoming a judge does not limit a man's career possibilities. Not a few American judges have resigned their posts to practice law (Botein, Peck, Rifkind) or to teach (Lawless, Hyde) or to run for high political office (Hughes, Taft). One man, George Edwards, even resigned from the Supreme Court of Michigan to become Police Commissioner of Detroit, and later resigned from that post to become a federal judge on the U.S. Court of Appeals. The interchangeability of capable lawyers is epitomized by the careers of Archibald Cox and Erwin Griswold. Cox left

[1] American Bar Foundation, *Statistical Report, supra*, p. 36, n. 3, at 103–171.

the Harvard law faculty, where he had been teaching labor law, to become Solicitor General of the United States, and as such, the principal advocate for the federal government in the Supreme Court of the United States. After a few years in the office he resigned to return to the Harvard faculty. A short time later, Griswold, who was Dean of the same school and a professor of taxation, resigned his job to take the one that had recently been vacated by Cox.

We regard the interchangeability of lawyers as a good feature of our system. It brings constantly fresh points of view into our courthouses, law offices and law schools, and it develops broad, statesmanlike competency in those who are capable and fortunate enough to move from job to job. It also relieves tedium.

CONTINUING EDUCATION OF THE BENCH AND BAR

During the last half century, one of the most interesting and significant developments in the legal profession has been the growth of formal educational programs for mature lawyers and judges. With the development of these programs, apprenticeship as a method of legal education at all levels has virtually disappeared.

Until the 1930's, apprenticeship was relied upon to fill the gap between law school and practice, but it proved to be unsatisfactory. Some young law school graduates went into law firms where, if they were lucky, they received high quality tutelage from older colleagues in the practical skills of the lawyer's art. Even so, the training they received was likely to be narrow rather than general, and not such as to fit them to perform a wide variety of legal tasks. Many law graduates were less fortunate, going immediately from law school into practice on their own, without guidance or practical training. The results were bad for themselves and for their clients. Still others went into government offices or into judicial clerkships, but their training also was likely to be specialized as well as of uneven quality. They were not taught to perform generally as lawyers. Furthermore, there was no method of insisting that the masters provide quality training to whatever apprentices they had—no method of policing the system.

Because of such deficiencies, efforts were made to find a better way than apprenticeship to bridge the gap between law school and practice. Dozens of programs sprung up simultaneously throughout the nation in which public spirited members of the bar tried to help their younger colleagues in the form of lectures on practical how-to-do-it subjects such as the drafting of routine agreements and the handling of simple, recurring situations. This movement received a great impetus when lawyers who had served in the armed forces during World War II were suddenly demobilized. They needed refresher courses to orient or re-orient themselves in the profession. Under the leadership of the American Law Institute and the American Bar Association, such programs were developed and made available not only to veterans but also to other lawyers who had not been in the armed forces.[1] It soon became evident that a significant proportion of all lawyers were interested in continuing legal education.

Continuing legal education has now become a regular feature of the American scene. Programs are given in every state of the union, each year reaching many thousands of lawyers. They are so numerous and diverse as to defy description. Some are for new lawyers to help them bridge the gap between law school and practice; others are for older lawyers to keep them abreast of the growth of the law. Some are for general practitioners; others are for specialists. The topics covered are as varied as the problems that lawyers are called upon to handle for their clients. The methods of presentation vary from lectures to seminars to demonstrations to panel discussions to sound films. Some of the programs last only a few hours while others last several days and still others several months. Some are sponsored by law schools, others by bar associations, others by organizations created

---

[1] See generally, National Conference on Continuing Legal Education, 'Position Paper' 146 (1967); Joint Committee on Continuing Legal Education, *Continuing Legal Education for Professional Competence and Responsibility* Ch. II (1958); *Report on the Joint Committee on Continuing Legal Education of the American Law Institute and the A.B.A.* (1964).

for the express purpose of carrying on legal education. Whatever the auspices, they make use of the services of practitioners, law professors and judges to give lectures and lead discussions.[1]

The most surprising aspect of continuing legal education is that it now extends to judges. Fifteen years ago, the thought of judges going back to school would have seemed ludicrous to most members of the profession. Now it is accepted as a matter of course. Occasionally one hears the statement that if a judge doesn't know how to be a judge when he goes on the bench, he should never have been elected or appointed, but this point of view is now hardly more than an echo from the past. Today, there is almost unanimous agreement that judges need special skills and attitudes that were not necessarily a part of their equipment as practicing lawyers, and that they can be helped to acquire these skills and attitudes in schools for judges. Those who are new to the bench are given an opportunity to orient themselves to responsibilities different from those they have known before. Experienced judges are given an opportunity to refresh their minds, to be made aware of new trends, to share ideas and insights with men facing problems which seem unique but are in fact common. The first program to be established on a more or less permanent basis was the Seminar for Appellate Judges, founded in 1956 at the New York University School of Law under the auspices of the Institute of Judicial Administration.[2] For two weeks each summer, 20 to 25 judges, drawn from state supreme courts and United States courts of appeals all over the nation, meet together under a combined faculty consisting of judges of long experience and law school professors. These men lead and stimulate discussion on current trends and developments in the law, opinion writing, court administration and a variety of other topics of special interest to appellate judges. Attendance is on a purely voluntary basis, but the seminar is so popular that

[1] Joint Committee on Continuing Legal Education, *Meeting the Educational Needs of the Newly Admitted Lawyer*, Ch. 3, Appendices B & D (1966).

[2] Burger, 'School for Judges', 33 F.R.D. 139 (1964); Leflar, 'The Appellate Judges Seminars', 21 Ark. L. Rev. and Bar Journal 190 (1967).

there are never quite enough places to accommodate all the judges who wish to come. The success of the seminars has led to the establishment of comparable programs for other judges. Among them is the National College of Trial Judges, offering month long programs for state judges exercising original jurisdiction, and the National College of Juvenile Court Judges, offering programs of three weeks' duration for judges handling juvenile cases. Scarcely any group of judges is neglected. There are seminars for federal judges, traffic court judges, even justices of the peace. Some are on a local basis, some on a state or regional or national basis.[1] One of the most recent to be established is the New York Academy of the Judiciary, operating under the auspices of the Institute of Judicial Administration. Its unique feature is an intensive two-week orientation program for newly appointed or elected judges in New York City, given to them on an individual tutorial basis before they ascend the bench. In all of these programs, law professors as well as senior judges participate.[2]

DISCIPLINE OF THE BAR AND THE BENCH

Just as admission to practice is a state, rather than a national, function, so also is discipline of the profession. Ordinarily the power to disbar, suspend or reprimand a lawyer who fails to live up to the canons of professional ethics is vested in the state supreme court. If the state bar association is 'integrated'—by which, in this context, we mean that membership in it is mandatory for all lawyers admitted to practice in the state—the court may delegate to it the power to conduct preliminary hearings and make recommendations in individual cases. If the only bar associations in the state are voluntary, the court ordinarily appoints its own committee of lawyers to perform these functions. More often than not, the lawyers so appointed are prominent members of voluntary bar associations.[3]

[1] Karlen, 'Judicial Education', 52 A.B.A.J. 1049 (1966); I.J.A., *Judicial Education in the U.S.*
[2] Gutman, 'An Experiment in Judicial Education', 52 Judicature 366 (1969).
[3] G. Winters, *Bar Association Organization and Activities* 6 (1954).

E

The rules of conduct for the profession, strangely enough, are not made by the state supreme court or any body of local lawyers, but derived from a code of ethics drafted and promulgated by the American Bar Association. The code has been adopted by statute or judicial decision, either expressly or implicitly, in all states.[1] It has recently been revised by the American Bar Association and is now known as the 'Code of Professional Responsibility.'

Stranger still, the American Bar Association is also responsible for the Canons of Judicial Ethics,[2] which are generally regarded as the standard for judicial conduct in the several states. However, machinery for their enforcement varies widely from state to state. In some states, the only method of getting rid of a judge who misbehaves is legislative impeachment and trial[3]—an exceedingly cumbersome. ill-defined and generally ineffective procedure. In other states, newer and better methods have been devised. For example, in New York there is a Court on the Judiciary which is convened specially as needed to hear claims of judicial misconduct and, if they are found justified, to decide whether the judge should be removed from office.[4] In California, there is a Commission on Judicial Qualifications, with a paid staff, to investigate similar charges, conduct hearings and make recommendations. Final authority to impose or withhold sanctions resides in the California Supreme Court.[5]

BAR ASSOCIATIONS

Having considered some of the activities of bar associations, the time has come to look at them as a whole. Great numbers of them are in existence and they are of all kinds. Some are organized

---

[1] *A.B.A. Canons of Professional Ethics* (1958); see also, O. Hood Phillips and P. McCoy, *Conduct of Judges and Lawyers* 7–20 (1952); see also, *A.B.A. Special Committee on Evaluation of Ethical Standards, Code of Professional Responsibility* (Preliminary Draft 1969).

[2] The Canons are now in process of revision by a high level committee of the A.B.A.

[3] Am. Jud. Soc. *Judicial Discipline and Removal*, Report No. 5 (April 1968).

[4] N.Y. Const. art. VI § 22.

[5] Calif. Const. art. VI § 10a; Calif. Code § 75060 (1964); see also, Frankel, 'The Commission on Judicial Qualifications', 36 Calif. S. Bar. J. 1008 (1962).

on a local—even neighbourhood basis, others on a state basis, others on a national, or even international, basis. In some, membership is voluntary, in others mandatory. Some are open only to women lawyers, others only to specialists in a limited area, such as those who practice in the federal courts.[1] The American Bar Association is a huge organization of some 145,000 lawyers, but membership is purely voluntary; and there is no formal connection between it and the various state and local bar associations. In combination, all these organizations correspond roughly to the English Law Society and Inns of Court, except for two important distinctions. First, we do not distinguish between barristers and solicitors; and second, our associations are designed not to fit a single system of justice, like that of England, but to fit the many separate systems of justice that prevail in a federal form of government. Whereas England has five professional organizations, we have literally hundreds of them.

The purposes of all these diverse organizations are, in general, two-fold: First, to promote the welfare of the legal profession itself; and second, to serve the public by improving laws and legal institutions in general. Under the first heading come such activities as improving legal education, regulating admission to the bar, preventing the unauthorized practice of law, setting schedules of minimum fees, establishing codes of ethics and disciplining lawyers who fail to live up to professional standards. The immediate impact of these activities is upon the legal profession itself, but their long range impact is upon the public at large, because they determine to a very large extent the quality of legal service that is available.

Other bar activities are only loosely connected with the profession as such. Some touch the profession tangentially, as where they are concerned with such matters as the selection of judges, the provision of legal assistance to indigents, the vesting of procedural rule making power in the courts and the prevention and control of crime. Others are aimed at matters of broad public

[1] See, e.g., *A.B.A. Bar Executive Key Handbook: Division of State and Local Bar Services* 1969.

concern which far transcend the legal profession, such as the regulation of firearms, electoral college reform and congressional ethics. In short, bar activities are not limited to professional concerns, but range over the entire spectrum of public affairs.[1]

LAW REFORM

Rather than discuss court reform activities of bar associations in isolation, I shall conclude this chapter by considering all of the agencies engaged in our multifarious efforts to improve the administration of justice.

In the United States, no one individual or agency is responsible for all the courts. There cannot be, for we do not have a single system of courts, but 50 separate state systems independent of each other, plus another federal system of courts. The federal system does not comprehend the state systems but runs parallel to them, with the only significant point of contact being the limited power of appellate review vested in the Supreme Court of the United States.[2] As pointed out in the first chapter, the Chief Justice of the United States is only symbolically the head of the American judiciary: neither he nor any other federal agency has any administrative control over the state courts.

Even within a single system of courts, responsibility for their overall operation is not concentrated in any single individual or group. This is as true of the federal courts as it is of the state courts; but for purposes of illustration, consider one of our better state systems, in which the courts are unified under centralized administrative control exercised by the chief justice of the highest appellate court in the state. The powers of such a chief justice are extremely limited compared to those exercised by the Lord Chancellor of England, and his responsibility is correspondingly small. He has no authority to appoint judges, or even to significantly affect their selection; he cannot be held

---

[1] 'The A.B.A. in Action', 55 A.B.A.J. 244 (1969); see also, O. Marden, The President's Annual Address, 'The Organized Bar—Today and Tommorow', 53 A.B.A.J. 801 (1967).

[2] See generally, *supra*, Ch. 1.

responsible therefore for the way they perform their duties. He has no authority to act as a legislator; he cannot, therefore, be held responsible for the quality of many of the basic ground rules by which the courts must operate. He has no authority to participate in the executive branch of government in which the all important budgetary decisions are made; he cannot, therefore, be held responsible for the adequacy of the personnel and physical facilities furnished to the courts. All the chief justice can do is work with whatever materials are given him by agencies beyond his control.

Because of the lack of concentrated responsibility for the courts improving the administration of justice becomes everybody's business. Before considering other agencies outside of the legal profession, let us look at two examples of how concerted action between bar associations, the judiciary and other segments of the legal profession can accomplish major reforms.

Thirty-five years ago, civil procedure in the federal courts was in sad condition. There had still been no procedural merger between common law and equity and, while there was a uniform and moderately good procedure in equity cases, the procedure in common law actions varied from state to state, ranging in quality from bad to mediocre. The American Bar Association had been critical of the situation for years, and in 1934 finally managed to secure the passage of an Act of Congress which delegated rule making power to the Supreme Court of the United States.[1] The Court then proceeded to appoint an advisory committee, consisting of lawyers, judges and law professors, to assist in drafting a set of uniform, modern, simple rules of civil procedure. The reporter for the committee and the man who did most of the spadework was Charles E. Clark, who was then Professor of Law and Dean of Yale Law School, and who later became Chief Judge of the United States Court of Appeals for the Second Circuit. The committee labored for about three years to produce a final draft, but in the meantime

[1] Act of June 19, 1934, Ch. 651, §§ 1, 2, 48 Stat. 1064; see also, 28 U.S.C. § 2072.

circulated preliminary drafts to state and local bar associations and invited them, as well as individual lawyers and judges, to submit their views. In 1938 the job was finished and the rules were formally promulgated by the Supreme Court.[1] Since then, they have become a model for procedural reforms in many states, so that today about one half of the states have civil rules modelled after the federal pattern. In addition, the same technique used in promulgating the civil rules has been used also in amending them from time to time and has been successfully extended into other areas, such as criminal and appellate procedure.

The second example is more recent, involving the Institute of Judicial Administration. The Institute had been organized in 1952 chiefly through the efforts of Arthur T. Vanderbilt, who at various times in his career had been a practicing lawyer, a law professor and a judge, and who was probably the greatest figure our country has produced in the field of judicial administration. The Institute's membership was composed mostly of judges, but with a fair number of practicing lawyers and a few laymen as well. It was engaged (as it still is) in a broad program of research in judicial administration, but mostly on the civil side and centering to a considerable extent on the Minimum Standards of Judicial Administration which had been promulgated by the American Bar Association in 1938 when Vanderbilt was President.[2] In the early 1960's, the Institute became more concerned than it had been in the past about criminal justice in America, and decided to see what could be done in that then relatively neglected area. It hit upon the idea of formulating Minimum Standards of Criminal Justice; and, because its own resources were very limited, presented the idea to the American Bar Association as a project worthy of becoming the core of the Association's activities for the next few years. That is exactly what happened. The Association put up about a quarter of a million dollars of its own money and, with the help of the Institute, raised about half a million dollars more from two

---

[1] They are designated Federal Rules of Civil Procedure (F.R.C.P.).

[2] Vanderbilt, *Minimum Standards of Judicial Administration* (1949).

private foundations. The project was launched when the Association appointed an overall committee headed by J. Edward Lumbard, Chief Judge of the United States Court of Appeals for the Second Circuit to supervise the entire project, and six special committees to deal with various limited aspects of it. The committees were composed of distinguished judges, lawyers and law professors, and were given the assistance of other law professors who were hired to act as reporters in the same manner that Judge Charles Clark had acted as reporter to the Supreme Court's Advisory Committee on the Rules of Civil Procedure. The personnel of the various committees has changed from time to time. Chief Judge Lumbard was succeeded as chairman of the overall committee by Judge Warren E. Burger of the United States Court of Appeals for the District of Columbia. He later resigned when he was appointed Chief Justice of the United States, and was succeeded as chairman by U.S. District Judge William Jameson. Both Chief Justice Burger and Chief Judge Lumbard continue as honorary chairmen. The Institute of Judicial Administration acted as the Secretariat for the entire project, and coordinated the work of all the committees and all the reporters. The project is still going, but now in the process of being wound up. It has produced standards on a wide variety of criminal justice problems, which are published in ten volumes containing careful commentaries, and which have been approved by the general membership of the American Bar Association.[1] They are now available to all who are interested in improving the quality of criminal justice in state and federal courts. One of the topics was prejudicial publicity before and during trial. It seemed almost impossible to reconcile the constitutional right to a fair trial with the constitutional right to freedom of the press.[2] Because American courts, unlike those in England, were generally thought to be barred from proceeding directly against newsmen

---

[1] *A.B.A. Project on Minimum Standards for Criminal Justice: Fair Trial and Free Press; Post-Conviction Remedies; Pleas of Guilty; Appellate Review of Sentences; Speedy Trial; Providing Defense Services; Joinder and Severance; Sentencing Alternatives and Procedures; Trial by Jury.*

[2] U.S. Const. Amends. I, VI.

for contempt, the Committee on Fair Trial and Free Press decided to approach the problem in a different way. After prolonged study, it concluded that the wisest solution was to plug up the sources of information available to newsmen by prohibiting judges, prosecutors, defense lawyers and other law enforcement officials from talking to them about pending cases.[1] Other committees of the Minimum Standards project have dealt with equally difficult problems, and produced equally useful solutions. Their long range effect is only beginning to be felt, but is bound to be substantial.

Most, if not all, examples of large-scale efforts to improve the administration of justice in the United States involve active cooperation between all segments of the profession—not only judges and practicing lawyers, but also law professors. In fact, academic lawyers are especially useful in law reform work because they have more time to devote to it than most judges or practitioners, and they are likely to be more objective. Not being involved in the day to day chores of trying and deciding cases, they are less likely to become too busy to seek improvements or to develop myopia or to assume that whatever is familiar is also necessary.

Without dwelling further on professional involvement in law reform, let us turn to citizen involvement. Arthur T. Vanderbilt, of whom I have already spoken, thought more highly of ordinary citizens than he did of professionals in accomplishing judicial reform. When speaking of the reforms accomplished in New Jersey under his leadership, he was fond of saying that as long as he tried to work through lawyers and judges, nothing happened, and that it was only when he enlisted the support of such groups as the Gold Star Mothers and the Beekeepers Association that reform was accomplished. In commenting on the difficulty of securing reform in New York, he said it was apparent that such reform could only come, as it had in England and New Jersey,

---

[1] *A.B.A. Project on Minimum Standards, Standards Relating to Fair Trial and Free Press* (1968).

'through a popular movement of laymen led or advised by a few courageous and informed judges and lawyers'.[1] He gave substantially the same advice to the citizens of Illinois:

> 'If after several years of toil you do not succeed in getting what you want with the help of lawyers and judges, you will have to go over their heads or around them to the people.'[2]

Laymen are involved in a wide range of law reform efforts. The League of Women Voters and the Citizens Committee on the Courts, for example, are largely responsible for the simplification of court structure in New York in 1961. The Citizens Union in New York recently co-sponsored, along with the Institute of Judicial Administration, a series of public hearings on better methods of selecting judges. Citizens groups all over the country have been mobilized *ad hoc* by the American Judicature Society to press for improved methods of judicial selection and other needed improvements in the courts. The most substantial effort has been that spearheaded by the National Council on Crime and Delinquency, which has organized citizens at national, state and local levels to work on a continuing basis for better correctional facilities, improved probation and parole systems and, in general, more effective ways for preventing and controlling crime and juvenile delinquency. The accomplishments of the citizens working in these groups are substantial and worthy of high praise. They stimulate a hope that even more could be accomplished if some of the energies of these public spirited people could be channelled into the operation of our judicial system in much the same way that the energies of their English cousins are channelled into their magistrate system.

With all the law reform activity that I have been describing, one might be tempted to assume that our problems by now must be largely solved. That would be a mistake. Our courts are in a

---

[1] Vanderbilt, 'The Courts, The Public and the Bar' (Charles Evans Hughes Memorial Lecture delivered at New York County Lawyers' Association, Feb. 16, 1954).

[2] Vanderbilt, 'The Reorganization of the New Jersey Courts', 34 Chi. B. Record 161, 162 (1953).

state of crisis, as I shall try to demonstrate in the next chapter. The most affirmative thing that can be said is that our difficulties are being recognized and our problems are being defined, and a few of them solved. Those which remain are difficult, complex, stubborn and endlessly complicated by politics and self-interest. But at least we have learned what Judge Vanderbilt said long ago:

'Judicial reform is no sport for the short winded.'[1]

---

[1] Vanderbilt, *Minimum Standards, supra*, p. 54, n. 2 at xix.

Chapter 3   *Delay, Congestion, Crisis, Reform*

Having discussed in the two previous chapters the machinery of justice in the United States and the people who operate that machinery, in this chapter I propose to discuss the raw materials on which they work, their methods of dealing with those materials and the final product of their efforts, namely a certain kind of justice. In the earlier chapters I was mildly critical of American justice but mostly descriptive. In this one, I must be much more critical, for otherwise I would be guilty of distortion.

The raw materials are the cases brought to court. American courts are deluged with a heavy volume of cases, especially criminal cases. Against about 1,500,000 criminal prosecutions in England and Wales during the course of a year, the courts of New York State alone, which is the second largest of the 50 American states and which has a population one third the size of England and Wales, are confronted with about 5,700,000 criminal prosecutions, or almost four times as many. For both nations these figures include traffic offenses as well as ordinary crimes. If traffic offenses are excluded, the New York courts handle about 450,000 cases per year or about 80 per cent of the number of ordinary criminal cases handled by all courts of England and Wales combined (about 550,000 per year).[1] Turning to civil cases,

[1] Great Britain Home Office, *Criminal Statistics, England and Wales* 1966, xi; *Thirteenth Annual Report of the Administrative Board of the Judicial Conference of the State of New York*, 333, 335, 345, 346, 348, 383 (1968).

the courts of New York handle about 435,000 per year or about one fourth the number that are handled by the courts of England and Wales (about 1,800,000 per year).[1] In terms of cases per thousand of population, the civil caseload of New York is somewhat lighter and the criminal caseload considerably heavier than that of England and Wales.

It is fashionable to say that America is a lawless society and that Americans are more litigious than Englishmen. I doubt that this is true in view of the volume of civil litigation in England, and I doubt that the statement is a sufficient explanation of the volume of American criminal cases. I suspect that one of the reasons for congestion and delay in American courts is the malfunctioning of the judicial system itself.

The volume of cases in the United States is too great for the courts to handle in the way they presently operate. In some cities, it takes four or five years for a personal injury claim to be reached for trial, and in many other cities, two or three years.[2] In some cities, it takes a year or more for a criminal case to be reached.[3]

Delay, of course, is no newcomer to the law. It was condemned in the Magna Charta, criticized by Shakespeare and immortalized by Dickens in 'Bleak House'. About a century ago, a legislative committee in Massachusetts was pondering again the famous statement in the Magna Charta: 'to no one will we sell, to no one will we deny or delay right or justice.' Applying this to the situation in Massachusetts, the committee said:

> 'The barons compelled King John to bequeath this motto to our courts; it is engraved on their seals. . . . It is written in Latin in most of our courtrooms. It is well it is disguised in a dead language. If the delayed parties and witnesses who sit in the back seats could read it, they would disturb or break up the courts by the

[1] Lord Chancellor's Report, *Judicial Statistics, England and Wales, Civil Judicial Statistics.* 5 (1966); *Thirteenth Annual Report of the Administrative Board of the Judicial Conference of the State of New York*, 325, 335, 337, 339, 340, 344, 348, 383 (1968).

[2] Institute of Judicial Administration, *State Trial Courts of General Jurisdiction: Calendar Status Studies* (1953 through 1968).

[3] President's Commission on Law Enforcement and Administration of Justice, *The Challenge of Crime in a Free Society*, 127–129 (1967).

explosions of their laughter or their rage at the monstrous in-
congruity betwixt the theory and the practice.'[1]

Nevertheless, however bad delay may have been a century or
two ago, it is still very much with us today.

The United States has far more professional judges than
England, and far more lawyers;[2] and yet they are unable to keep
up with the work. One reason may be that America does not have
a magistrate system like England's. That gives England a large
reservoir of judicial manpower which can be tapped as needed.
Existing magistrates can be asked to work harder, and new
magistrates can be appointed whenever the occasion demands.[3]
It also contributes greatly to public understanding and acceptance
of the law, which in turn tends to prevent crime and so to cut
down the volume of prosecutions.

Another partial explanation of the congestion in American
courts is that they are a dumping ground for unsolved social
problems like homosexuality, alcoholism, narcotics addiction
and vagrancy. Not knowing what else to do with the offenders
(who happen also to be the victims), we haul them into court,
sentence them to jail for a while, and then send them away
uncured. Usually nothing has been accomplished except to
clog court calendars. I believe that English courts have been
and probably still are saddled with similar problems.

There is another type of social-judicial problem, however,
which is peculiarly American. It involves the application of
constitutional principles to areas where English courts seldom
venture—racial integration in the schools[4] and the equalization
of voting rights,[5] to cite two familiar examples. It is not the

---

[1] Quoted in *II Selected Writings of Arthur T. Vanderbilt* 110 (ed. F. Klein & J. Lee 1967).

[2] See *supra*, Ch. 2.

[3] See generally, Jackson, *The Machinery of Justice in England*, Ch. IV (5th ed. 1967).

[4] *Brown* v. *Board of Education*, 347 U.S. 483 (1954).

[5] *Baker* v. *Carr*, 369 U.S. 186 (1962). Decisions, such as this one and the school segregation case (*Supra*, n. 4), are not necessarily wise in the long run. See 1969 *Holmes Lectures at Harvard Law School*, delivered by Prof. Alexander M. Bickel of Yale (discussed on editorial page of N.Y. Times, Oct. 10, 1969).

Supreme Court of the United States alone that is concerned with such problems. All courts at all levels are required to implement its decisions.[1] This consumes a substantial amount of judicial time which can ill be spared from traditional tasks. Perhaps the blame for this diversion of judicial energy rests less upon the courts than upon legislatures for their failure to come to grips with pressing social problems. No matter who is to blame for leaving such problems to the courts, a toll is exacted against the judicial system in terms of the judicial time which must be spent in resolving them.

Finally, there is the large area of litigation created by the automobile where the courts are grappling with problems that seem too big for them, that do not fit comfortably into traditional patterns of civil or criminal litigation, and that might better be entrusted to administrative agencies. A large part of the time of the courts is devoted to prosecutions for traffic offenses, including parking violations. The cumbersome machinery of the criminal law is invoked to deal with activities which are not regarded by most people as truly criminal and which could more easily and efficiently be handled by clerks in motor vehicle bureaus collecting fixed penalties for parking violations and similar infractions as a condition of renewing operators' licenses or motor vehicle registrations.[2] An even larger chunk of judicial time is devoted to civil actions for damages arising out of auto accidents. Here the complicated, slow and expensive machinery of civil litigation is invoked to administer payments under what most citizens regard as an unsatisfactory and uncertain insurance scheme.[3] Industrial accident claims were once handled the same way, with similar delays and similar injustices, but now they are channeled into Workmen's Compensation Boards under new, simpler and more sensible substantive and procedural rules. A

---

[1] Fleischer, 'Study of Circumvention: The Enforceability of "Brown," 41 Denver L. Cen. J. 165 (1964).

[2] See e.g., Traffic Court Reform, 4 Col. J. of Law & Social Problems 255 (1968).

[3] Walter E. Meyer Research Institute of Law, *Dollars, Delay and the Automobile Victim*, I & II (1968).

growing body of opinion in the United States contends that much the same thing should be done with auto accident claims,[1] but until that happens—and it can happen only by legislative action— the courts will continue to be heavily burdened with them.

As if the courts didn't have enough to keep them busy, our system encourages litigation.

First, let us look at costs. With few exceptions, we do not allow the winning party in a lawsuit to collect his reasonable attorney's fees from the losing party, even if the loser's claim or defense was wholly unfounded.[2] Despite the obvious unfairness of making a man pay legal fees for a contest which ought never to have taken place, we defend our practice on the ground that it keeps the courthouse doors open, so that anyone may assert any legal right that he thinks he has, without fear of any serious penalty if it turns out to be without substance. The courthouse doors are indeed kept open wide, but is that a legitimate goal when the courthouse is already crowded to capacity?

Let us consider next contingent fees. It is common, in fact customary, for a lawyer to undertake a personal injury or wrongful death claim upon the agreement that he will receive no fee if the client loses, but a percentage of the recovery if he wins—often one third.[3] Sometimes the lawyer advances out-of-pocket expenses for the litigation without any agreement that the client will reimburse him if the case is lost, and there are even cases where the lawyer has been known to pay medical expenses and living costs for the client while the action is pending.[4] This

[1] Keeton & O'Connell, *Basic Protection for the Traffic Victim*, 127–139 (1965).

[2] Note, 'Attorneys' Fees: Where Shall the Ultimate Burden Lie?', 20 Vand. L. Rev. 1216 (1967). For examples of exceptions to the general rule, see: 15 U.S.C. § 15 (1964) (antitrust suits); 17 U.S.C. § 116 (1964) (copyright cases); 28 U.S.C. § 2678 (1964) (tort claims against U.S.); 35 U.S.C. § 285 (1964) (patent cases).

[3] F. B. MacKinnon, *Contingent Fees for Legal Services*, 65–66 (1964); Defense Research Institute, 'A Study of Contingent Fees in the Prosecution of Personal Injury Claims', 33 Insurance Counsel J. 197 (1966)

[4] Botein, 'Accident Fraud Investigation' (Report to the Appellate Division of the Supreme Court 1st Judicial Dept., the Assoc. of the Bar of the City of N.Y., the N.Y. County Lawyers' Ass'n, and Hon. Wm. Copeland, D.A. of N.Y. County 1953).

partnership arrangement is a gamble, but if victory comes, it sometimes pays off handsomely for the lawyer, because the verdict may run into hundreds of thousands of dollars. Contingent fees entail other evils beside court congestion. As Judge Learned Hand remarked: 'It is hard to expect lawyers who are half litigants to forego the advantages which come from obscuring the case and supporting contentions which they know to be false.' He went on to say: 'As a litigant, I should dread a lawsuit beyond almost anything else short of sickness and death.'[1] Contingent fee arrangements also occur in other types of litigation, notably derivative stockholders' actions, where the successful lawyer's fee is measured by the benefit he has conferred on all members of the class he purports to represent.[2] Many of them, of course, have never heard of him. As one might imagine, some American lawyers are busy and prosperous entrepreneurs, always ready to provide business for the courts. Viewing contingent fees in their most favorable aspect, they make legal representation possible for some poor people in some situations where they might otherwise not be able to hire lawyers.

Aid to indigents does not stop with contingent fees. Happily, there are sounder forms of legal assistance available. We have neighbourhood law offices, public defender offices and legal aid societies,[3] whose functions are to provide legal services for the poor. As I pointed out in the last chapter, these agencies have their drawbacks too, but no one could seriously doubt that they are far superior to contingent fee arrangements. In the field of criminal law, free legal representation for those who cannot afford to pay is required by the Constitution of the United States, as interpreted by the Supreme Court.[4] While legal aid in all its forms undoubtedly entails more work for the courts, no responsible person would wish it any other way. The poor, in

---

[1] Hand, '3 Lectures on Legal Topics', 89, 104–105.

[2] Kalven and Rosenfield, 'The Contemporary Function of the Class Suit', 8 U. of Chicago L. Rev. 684 (1941).

[3] See *supra*, Ch. 2.

[4] *Gideon* v. *Wainwright*, 372 U.S. 335 (1963).

other words, have as much right as the rich to the time of the courts.

Let us turn, therefore, to other reasons why the courts are kept busy by the rich and the poor alike. A major reason is the unpredictability of the results of litigation. I do not mean merely that there are many unsettled areas in American law just as there are in English law, but rather that we have special, unique sources of uncertainty in the law. We take the doctrine of 'stare decisis' far less seriously than the English do, so that almost any previous decision is subject to reconsideration at any time. This is true not only of constitutional interpretations, but also of statutory construction and common law rules.[1] Is there a rule giving immunity to charitable organizations from tort liability? Never mind; it may be eliminated in the next case. Is there a rule allowing actions for breach of promise of marriage? Never mind; it may be changed when the defendant argues his case in the state supreme court. Such are the attitudes of lawyers. The attitudes of judges are not much different. They are not content to let legislatures make changes in the law, but feel impelled themselves to make changes when legislatures are too slow in acting.[2] Even a newly declared legislative rule does not settle the law. It is subject to challenge for constitutional infirmity, and subject also to judicial interpretation.

Another factor making for uncertainty is the federal system, allowing all 50 states as well as the central government to have legislative and judicial powers of their own. It is often exceedingly difficult to know in advance what law will be applied in a particular case. Our conflict of laws rules, or as they are sometimes called, rules of 'private international law', are voluminous, complicated, uncertain and unpredictable. Until the present century, they may have been complicated and arbitrary, but at least they yielded generally predictable results. Now they are being recast into vague concepts of uncertain application. For example, in a

[1] See *supra*, Ch. 1.
[2] Schaefer, 'Precedent and Policy', 34 U. of Chicago L. Rev. 3 (1966); also see *supra*, Ch. 1.

F

tort case, the old rule was that the defendant ordinarily had to be sued in a state where he could be personally served with a summons. The new concept is that he can be sued in any state with which he has had sufficient 'contact' to make it 'reasonable' and consistent with 'traditional notions of fair play and substantive justice' to require him to defend.[1] The old choice of law rule in such a case was that the substantive law of the place where the tort occurred would govern. The new concept is that the court of the forum will follow the law of the state having the most 'significant contacts' with the litigation.[2] The difficulties posed by such concepts in a nation where each state retains a high degree of sovereignty and where people travel from state to state very freely are formidable. They add new elements of instability to laws which are already uncertain, and make confusion worse confounded.

The final and possibly the most important factor in making litigation unpredictable is the jury. Its very large role in the decision making process is constitutionally guaranteed. Whereas the civil jury has virtually disappeared in England, we use juries in a wide variety of civil cases, particularly personal injury and wrongful death claims.[3] We also use juries far more extensively than England does in criminal cases, for most of our criminal cases of any seriousness are tried in the superior courts,[4] while such cases in England are tried summarily by magistrates. Juries almost inevitably bring a large element of uncertainty into any courtroom. They are supposed to be governed by law, but often they cannot understand the instructions they receive from judges.[5] Furthermore, juries tend to regard themselves as miniature legislatures,

[1] See e.g. *International Shoe Co.* v. *Washington*, 326 U.S. 910 (1945); *McGee* v. *International Life Insurance Co.*, 355 U.S. 220 (1957).

[2] See e.g., *Pearson* v. *Northeast Airlines, Inc.*, 309 F. 2nd 553 (2nd Cir. 1962); *Babcock* v. *Jackson*, 12 N.Y. 2d 473, 191 N.E. 2d 279, N.Y.S. 2d (1963); see also, 'Comments on *Babcock* v. *Jackson*, A Recent Development in Conflict of Laws', 63 Col. L. Rev. 1212 (1963).

[3] See *supra*, Ch. 2.

[4] Cf. *Duncan* v. *Louisiana*, 88 S. Ct. 1444 (1968).

[5] Green, 'Juries and Justice—The Jury's Role in Personal Injury Cases', 1962 Univ. of Ill. L. Forum 152; see also *supra*, Ch. 2.

applying whatever rules they consider necessary to achieve just results.[1] No wonder, then, that hardly any case is considered by lawyers too hopeless to bring or defend so long as it is destined to go before a jury. The only thing they seem to worry about is whether they can 'get to the jury', indicating their belief that the law and the facts are relatively unimportant.

Closely related to the volume of litigation in understanding the demands made on judicial time is the way that cases are handled.

Just finding the law is a difficult and time consuming operation. This is not only because of the inherent uncertainties in the law which I have just discussed, but also because of the form of our judge-made law. All the opinions of our appellate courts and a goodly number of trial court opinions as well are published, not just a few as in England, selected because of their importance as precedents.[2] For New York State alone, there are over 900 thick volumes of reports now in existence, and they are continuing to pour off the presses at the rate of 12 to 15 new volumes a year. However, to have a minimum working library of domestic law, a practitioner or judge would have to possess not only all those volumes but also all the United States Supreme Court reports—approximately 400 volumes now, and growing at the rate of four volumes a year. That is because federal law, within its limited sphere, and as interpreted by the Supreme Court, is equally binding within the state.[3] If one wanted to have available all published decisions of all state and federal courts (and, because of our federal system, any of the decisions might become relevant in a local case), he would have to acquire a library of over 5,000 volumes and be prepared to add to it at the rate of over 100 additional volumes each year—more than any lawyer could hope to read even if he spent full time at the job. This does not include statutes or administrative regulations, nor does it include treatises,

[1] *Skidmore* v. *Baltimore & O. R. Co.*, 167 F. 2d 54 (2nd Cir. 1948).

[2] Karlen, *Appellate Courts in the United States and England*, 99–104, 110, 129 (1963).

[3] U.S. Const. art. VI.

digests, formbooks, law reviews or similar non-authoritative sources of the law. Because of the plethora of published decisions, computers are beginning to be used to search for cases in point. No lawyer or judge can hope to know all the law of the United States. He does well to know the law of his own state in broad terms. When he is confronted with a specific problem, he must go to the books, with or without the aid of a computer, and there he is likely to find more decisions than he cares to read. Dozens of decisions are cited to American courts where one would do in England. Worse still, the courts themselves get into the same habit and cite cases which are at best superfluous and probably worse—confusing. Thus American case law grows and grows until one wonders whether it is not about to topple of its sheer bulk and weight. Yet no relief is in sight. We have no Law Commission as in England working on codification of all the law. Our closest approach is the American Law Institute, a private organization, attempting to restate the law in various fields by distilling from the multitudinous decisions of the courts of the 50 states general principles of wide application.[1] But these re-statements are not even attempting to wipe the slate clean. The one thing we can be sure they are doing is providing additional citations to bedevil lawyers and judges.

Finding facts is as difficult as finding the law. This is because we are bound by rules of evidence which tongue-tie witnesses and screen out sources of information that are regarded everywhere except in court as at least trustworthy enough to be considered. These rules persist chiefly because we insist upon using juries while at the same time distrusting their capacity to separate the wheat from the chaff. The rules are archaic, unduly complicated, and about as helpful as the common law forms of action were. They consume much time at trial and upon appeal. Yet again relief is hardly in sight. A Model Code of Evidence was prepared some

---

[1] H. Goodrich and P. Wolkin, *The Story of the American Law Institute 1923–1961*, 5–18 (1961); see also, American Law Institute, *Annual Reports* (1959–1968); American Law Institute, *Annual Meetings Proceedings*.

25 years ago,[1] but it could not overcome professional apathy and resistance. A modified version of the reform advocated in the Model Code, but far less sweeping, was embodied in the so-called Uniform Rules of Evidence, drafted by the Commissioners on Uniform Law. These rules have been adopted only in three states and then in somewhat changed form, so that the rules presently in force throughout the country are anything but uniform.[2] An advisory committee to the Supreme Court of the United States in its procedural rule making capacity is urging a reform for the federal courts based upon the uniform rules, but this is the most helpful development on the horizon. If adopted, the new rules will govern in the federal courts, but will have only the force of example for the several states.

Evidence is particularly troublesome in criminal cases, where the traditional rules have been complicated by a series of constitutional decisions by the Supreme Court of the United States related to the admissibility of illegally obtained evidence[3] and confessions.[4] Because of these decisions, the lower courts are required to spend much of their time on tangential inquiries little related to finding out what the defendant did and what should be done about him. These inquiries relate mostly to whether the accused's rights have been adequately protected— particularly whether the police have acted properly. We seem to have gotten off the main track, to have lost interest in finding out whether the accused is guilty of the crime charged against him. Guilt may be all but conceded by defense counsel, who nevertheless argue—and often successfully—against conviction on the ground that some piece of evidence against the accused was illegally obtained, or that he confessed before he had the assistance of a lawyer, or that his constitutional rights were compromised in some other way. The criminal goes free because

[1] American Law Institute, *Model Code of Evidence, Introduction* (1942).

[2] *Uniform Rules of Evidence;* see also, *Handbook of the National Conference of Commissioners on Uniform State Laws. . . .* 1967, chart, ff. p. 162.

[3] E.g. *Mapp* v. *Ohio,* 367 U.S. 643 (1961).

[4] E.g., *Miranda* v. *Arizona,* 384 U.S. 436 (1966).

the constable has blundered, to paraphrase a famous statement of Benjamin Cardozo in summarizing the effect of the Supreme Court decisions of which I have been speaking.[1] Since these decisions now apply to state as well as federal courts,[2] all courts at all levels are required to spend much of their time deciding whether the rules of detection, investigation, arrest and prosecution have been observed.

There is much debate as to whether these decisions of the Supreme Court have contributed to lawlessness in the United States. Critics claim that the Court coddles criminals and makes law enforcement more difficult than it ought to be. Supporters of the Court say this is nonsense—that nobody about to commit rape is thinking about whether a confession can be used against him, or calculating the advisability of claiming his privilege against self-incrimination. True enough, but is that a sufficient answer? Each decision, standing alone, seems to be an attempt to make the criminal law more humane and to see that no person accused of crime is treated unfairly or denied the equal protection of the law. But when the decisions are viewed together in their totality, they take on a different aspect. Their combined effect is to set free many persons whose guilt is not seriously in doubt, including gangsters and professional criminals, and at the same time to slow down some cases by making necessary the tangential inquiries of which I have been speaking, while speeding up other cases by the sheer pressure of calendar congestion. The result is anything but the equal justice aimed at. Ordinary men in the street are aware of these results even though they do not understand the reasoning behind the decisions themselves. My own view, which I cannot support by any evidence and which is by no means shared by all American lawyers, is that the Supreme Court decisions, while not directly responsible for lawlessness, have contributed to a widespread, popular belief that people can 'get away with anything.' That belief—coupled with public misunderstanding of correctional goals and techniques, particularly

[1] *People* v. *Defore*, 242 N.Y. 13, 21, 150 N.E. 585, 588 (1926).
[2] *Supra.* p. 69, nn. 3 and 4.

the failure of many people to understand the desirability of individualized punishment and the purpose of probation and parole—leads to the feeling that criminal law is neither swift nor sure nor powerful, but only a paper tiger, not to be feared. That feeling, it seems to me, cannot help but break down inhibitions against committing crimes of all sorts. It may even contribute a special American flavor to the world-wide movement of outright defiance of law by student radicals and assorted anarchists who seem bent on destroying the society in which they live. If so, increasing crime must add to the ever increasing burdens of the courts.

A feature of our procedure that slows down civil as well as criminal cases is the use of juries. I have already discussed how they add to the uncertainty of the law. My point now is that they also lengthen the time needed to dispose of cases. Countless courtroom hours are spent in selecting and instructing juries, but that is not all. The trial process itself is markedly slowed down by the presence of a jury. Former Judge David W. Peck of New York estimated that a jury trial took on the average about three times as much courtroom time as a trial before a judge alone[1]. That was probably a conservative estimate because he did not take account of the fact that a new trial is frequently ordered after a jury verdict, either because the presiding judge is dissatisfied with the result, or because an appellate court finds some error in the proceedings. New trials in cases tried by judges alone are comparatively rare.

Another cause of delay in both civil and criminal cases is adjournments. They are freely asked and freely granted. Since our legal profession is not split between barristers and solicitors and since we do not believe that an advocate can be expected on a moment's notice to try a case that has been prepared by someone else, any lawyer who pleads a previous engagement or who has been recently substituted as counsel

---

[1] 'Jury Trial on Trial—A Symposium', 28 N.Y.S.B. Bulletin 322, 338 (1956); see also, M. Green, 'Juries and Justice', *supra*, p. 66, n. 5; H. Zeisel, H. Kalven, Jr. & B. Buchholz, *Delay in the Courts* 94–103 (1959).

can expect a very sympathetic hearing when he asks for an
adjournment. A case in point is that of James Earl Ray, when
he was awaiting trial in Tennessee on the charge that he had
assassinated Martin Luther King. Ray was arrested in England
in June of 1968 and taken to Memphis for trial. A lawyer of his
own choice prepared his defense, but when the trial was scheduled
to begin in mid-November, Ray dismissed that lawyer and
retained another. The new lawyer appeared in court and asked a
further delay so that he could prepare the case. The adjournment
was granted—for about four months, until March of 1969. Then
Ray pleaded guilty. Had he not done so, his new lawyer might
well have asked and received another adjournment.

Finally, we come to proceedings after trial. It is standard
American practice to allow at least one appeal as of right from
any judgment, civil or criminal. There is little or no screening to
discover quickly the appeals which are without substance and
dispose of them summarily. Instead, the usual assumption is that
all are worthy of full deliberation by a slow and cumbersome
process. It involves the preparation of a record of trial of the
proceedings below, the exchange of written arguments (called
'briefs') between the attorneys, the study of those documents by
all members of the appellate court, an oral argument, a preliminary conference between the judges as to their tentative decision,
the preparation of an opinion for the court and possibly of
dissenting and concurring opinions as well, and finally, the
promulgation of the court's decision. All this takes many months
from the rendition of the original trial court judgment, and
sometimes years elapse before the decision of the appellate court
is announced.[1] Not infrequently, there are still further appeals.
Some states have intermediate appellate courts as well as supreme
courts,[2] and above the state supreme court there is the Supreme
Court of the United States for federal questions. Appeals beyond
the first level are usually entertained only in the discretion
of the next court, but that does not prevent some cases from

[1] Karlen, *Appellate Courts in the United States and England*, 154 (1963).
[2] XVII Book of the States 107 (1968).

going through three levels of appeal. For example, an appeal from a trial court in New York might go first to the Appellate Division of that state, then to the Court of Appeals, which is the state's highest court, then finally to the Supreme Court of the United States. At each level, the procedure would be substantially the same, with the delays that I have indicated. Moreover, at each stage, there would be the possibility of a rehearing with still further delay.

Successive stages of appellate review occur not only in civil cases but also in criminal cases. Whereas in England criminal appeals to the House of Lords are comparatively rare, in the United States successive criminal appeals are common.[1] The United States Supreme Court, for example, hears about half as many criminal appeals as civil appeals.[2] Furthermore, criminal appeals in the United States often result in new trials. If an error is discovered in the proceedings below which the appellate court thinks was prejudicial to the rights of the accused, or a violation of his constitutional rights, the case is remanded to be tried again. Indeed, although appellate courts do not admit this openly, they sometimes strain to find error in a conviction when what they are really objecting to is a sentence beyond their power of review, and they sometimes hold an error to be prejudicial chiefly because they want to discipline the trial judge and induce him to mend his ways in future cases. We do not follow the English practice of weighing the effect of an error very carefully and then, if it is really harmless, affirming the judgment. Instead, we find prejudice easily and grant new trials freely. I am not suggesting that we should follow the English practice of freeing the defendant when the judgment must be reversed because of a prejudicial error, but only that we should be less profligate in the granting of new trials.

Appeals in criminal cases are likely to increase in the near future rather than decrease. One reason is that lawyers are being made

[1] Karlen, *Appellate Courts in the United States and England*, 147 (1963).

[2] E.g., *Summary of the 1967–68 Supreme Court Term*, 82 Harvard L. Rev. 63, 308–309 (1969).

available to indigents on a greater scale than ever before at both trial and appellate levels. Another reason is that sentencing is coming under appellate scrutiny to a greater extent than in the past. The traditional practice, which is still followed in well over half of the states, is to limit appellate review to the legality of sentences and to allow trial courts unrestricted discretion in fixing sentences within the limits allowed by statute.[1] Now, however, there is a growing demand for appellate review of the discretionary element in sentencing, much along the lines followed by England for the last 60 years.[2] There is also an increasing tendency to challenge the constitutionality of severe sentences, chiefly on the ground that they entail 'cruel and unusual punishment' in violation of the Eighth Amendment to the United States Constitution.

Extensive proceedings after trial are likely to be more common in criminal cases than in civil cases because of the existence of collateral post-conviction remedies. After a man has been convicted in a state trial court and appealed his case as far as he can go, he can still sue out what is confusingly called either a 'writ of habeas corpus' or a 'writ of corum nobis', or some statutory substitute, to test whether he is being illegally detained because of some violation of his constitutional rights during the earlier proceedings.[3] This new attack on the judgment, often involving a lengthy hearing and the taking of much evidence, is heard before a single judge in a state trial court, whose judgment may then be appealed all the way up again. If the conviction is still standing, the accused may start all over again with another, similar habeas corpus proceeding before another single judge in a federal court, then if the court's ruling is adverse, appeal again to a United States Court of Appeals, and finally, seek, and possibly get final review in the Supreme Court of the United States. He

[1] Brewster, 'Appellate Review of Sentences,' 40 F.R.D. 79 (1966).

[2] Karlen, *Appellate Courts, supra*, p. 67, n. 2, at 111, 147–148; see also, *A.B.A. Project on Minimum Standards, Standards Relating to Appellate Review of Sentencing* (1968).

[3] 28 U.S.C. § 2254 (1964); see also, Carter, 'The Use of Federal Habeas Corpus by State Prisoners', 4 Am. Crim. L. Quart. 20 (1965).

would have then gone all the way to the top three times, in each instance through successive layers of appellate courts. If he happened to be indigent, all this maneuvering would have been done at no cost to himself, and more than likely subsidized by public funds. The notorious case of Caryl Chessman was kept going for 12 years between the time of his conviction for murder, and his execution.[1] Another case in point is that of Edgar H. Smith, Jr., who has now been in Death Row in New Jersey for 11 years. He was convicted in 1957 for the murder of a 15 year old girl. After three unsuccessful attempts to appeal to the Supreme Court of the United States, his fourth appeal, on federal habeas corpus, resulted in an order that the court below should reconsider its decision to deny Smith a full hearing on his claim that an illegal confession had been admitted at his trial. His contention is that he confessed to the police in jail after he had been indicted and without his assigned lawyer being present. This, he says, violates a decision of the Supreme Court made some seven years after his original conviction.[2] Doubtless his case still has a long time to go; and he may break Chessman's record.

Criminal cases tried in the federal courts cannot be dragged out quite so long. They can only be appealed within the federal system and then reviewed again by habeas corpus within the same system.[3] Even so, the post-conviction proceedings are far more drawn out than anything that would be tolerated in England.

Perhaps these elaborate post-conviction proceedings are good therapy for prisoners, giving them an opportunity to be heard on their grievances, whether real or fancied. Perhaps they do no harm in the cases where they are used, since they occur when the prisoners are in custody serving their sentences. Nevertheless, they consume judicial time which otherwise could be devoted to new cases and which is badly needed if those cases are to be handled

---

[1] Cf. *People* v. *Chessman*, 52 Cal. 2d 467, 341 P. 2d 679, 701–705 (1959).

[2] N.Y. Times, Nov. 13, 1968, p. 24, col. 1.

[3] 28 U.S.C. § 2255.

properly. There must be some better form of therapy than non-stop litigation—something less harmful to the rights of other litigants. Unfortunately, however, there is no sustained, serious effort in the United States to get rid of post-conviction proceedings—only sporadic grumblings. Instead, the tendency is to regularize and institutionalize them.[1] Perhaps a better solution for the legitimate grievances of prisoners will be found in appellate review of sentences, a development now on the horizon.

Americans seem to think no more highly of the doctrine of *res judicata* than of the doctrine of *stare decisis*, at least so far as criminal cases go. We seem to be driven by some inner compulsion never to let a case rest, or a rule of law lie undisturbed. No judge, however loud his protestations of respect for other judges, seems to be willing to trust any other judge; he must see for himself that justice has been done. Needless to say, all this takes a great deal of time.

The delays that I have been describing before, during and after trial inure to the benefit of defendants in both civil and criminal cases. Why should an insurance company settle a personal injury claim when it knows that the case may not be reached for trial for several years? In the meantime, witnesses who could prove the plaintiff's case may forget or disappear; and the plaintiff himself may die. Why should the accused in a criminal prosecution plead guilty? More than likely he is free on bail or on his own recognizance, for this is becoming more and more the practice in the United States; he is probably well advised by counsel, supplied at public expense; and he knows that the case will not be reached for trial for six months or a year, possibly longer. The prosecution witnesses may forget or disappear, and the victim of the crime may become so disgusted with delays and adjournments that he will drop the charges if he can or fail to appear at the trial when it is finally reached. It is even possible that the Supreme Court of the United States may discover a new constitutional right

[1] *A.B.A. Project on Minimum Standards for Criminal Justice, Standards Relating to Post-Conviction Remedies* (1967).

for the accused. This is not intended as a snide remark, but as a sober description of why many cases are deliberately delayed. Because delay yields such rich dividends, it pays to demand a trial, quite apart from the chance of winning the case either at the trial or the appellate level. The 'guarantee' of a speedy trial contained in the federal and in most state constitutions is phrased in terms of a right possessed by those accused of crime. The plain fact of the matter, however, is that most defendants don't want a speedy trial. What they more often desire is as much delay as possible for the reasons I have just described. It is the public interest which usually suffers from delay in criminal cases.

Delays beget further delays. Pleas of guilty are becoming fewer, and trials are increasing. The result is that court calendars are becoming more congested than ever, and overall delay increases. This is ominous, because the only chance that courts have with their present inflow of cases and their present manpower is to dispose of as many of them as possible without trial—by pleas of guilty in criminal cases and settlements in civil cases.

Delay is an evil in itself, but it leads to other evils, even more serious. When criminal justice is neither swift nor certain, the deterrent effect of the criminal law is lost. Crime increases and the conditions of living, particularly in the cities, deteriorate. A Presidential Commission reported in 1969 that:

> The existence of crime, the talk about crime, the reports of crime, and the fear of crime have eroded the basic quality of life of many Americans. A Commission study conducted in high crime areas of two large cities found that:
>
> 43 per cent of the respondents say they stay off the streets at night because of their fear of crime.
>
> 35 per cent say they do not speak to strangers any more because of their fear of crime.
>
> 21 per cent say they use cars and cabs at night because of their fear of crime.
>
> 20 per cent say they would like to move to another neighborhood because of their fear of crime.
>
> The findings of the Commission's national survey generally

support those of the local surveys. One-third of a representative sample of all Americans say it is unsafe to walk alone at night in their neighborhoods. Slightly more than one-third say they keep firearms in the house for protection against criminals. Twenty-eight per cent say they keep watchdogs for the same reason.[1]

When civil justice is unduly delayed, people lose faith that the courts can resolve their disputes and they sense a widening gap between what they consider social justice and what they see going on in the courts.

A tragic casualty of undue delay is the ideal of equal justice under law. When civil and criminal cases pile up to the extent that they now have in the United States, the judical machinery becomes so overburdened that it cannot produce equal justice for all. Instead, it begins to yield unequal injustice for all. This leads to a paradox which is hard to explain. Not all cases are handled in slow motion. Some are speeded up to a frantic pace by assembly line methods. If you were to walk into a courtroom in New York City where traffic offenses and similar minor charges were being processed, you would be dismayed. The courtroom would be crowded to capacity, with defendants, police officers, witnesses, bailiffs, clerks and spectators milling around in great confusion, and spilling out into the corridors. The noise would be so loud that you would not be able to hear what was going on in the front of the courtroom. If you jostled your way forward to a place near the bench, you would discover that pleas of guilty were being received and sentences imposed at the rate of about one case a minute. A few cases would be dismissed and a few others tried, but ordinarily after the pleas had been disposed of. Trials would take a little, but not much, longer than pleas, because they would consist mainly of explanations by the defendants of why they had committed the offenses charged against them. As an experienced observer of criminal courts throughout the country said: 'For most defendants in the criminal process, there is scant regard for them as individuals. They are numbers on

[1] President's Commission on Law Enforcement and the Administration of Justice, Challenge of Crime v. vi, *supra*, p. 60, n. 3.

dockets, faceless ones to be processed and sent on their way.'[1] Too often they do not understand what is happening to them or why.

After that spectacle, you might be tempted to step into another courtroom down the corridor where more serious cases were being arraigned. The scene before you would be much like the one you just left, but the pace would be a little slower. Each case might take three or four minutes. The courtroom would be a little more crowded, however, because district attorneys, legal aid attorneys, private attorneys and bail bondsmen would be present to swell the ranks of people such as those you saw in the other courtroom. The judge would not be imposing sentence, but only dismissing some cases and taking pleas in others. Many of the pleas would be 'guilty', but to lesser offenses than those originally charged and carrying lighter penalties.[2] When a plea of guilty was entered, the judge would fix a date for sentencing, but if a plea of not guilty was entered, he would fix a date for trial. In either event, he would release the defendant on bail or his own recognizance, or order him into custody. If you investigated why the judge was accepting pleas to lesser offenses so readily, you would discover that such pleas were the result of bargaining between defendants and the district attorney's office. In other words, it is customary for the lawyers on both sides to get together and decide what punishment, if any, is appropriate in a particular case, and for the judge to go along with whatever arrangement is made. Plea bargaining is no secret, under-the-table operation. It is a well recognized and openly acknowledged procedure. Here is how it works in a concrete case, as described by a former New York prosecutor:

> William Townes, one April half a dozen years ago, at knife-point forced a woman he accosted in her building hallway to admit him to her apartment. Once there, he forced her to undress, speeding the process by cutting part of her clothing from her body. When,

[1] E. Barrett, Jr., 'Criminal Justice, The Problem of Mass Production' in *The Courts, the Public and the Law Explosion* 85, 87 (ed. H. W. Jones, 1965).
[2] Cf. *A.B.A. Project on Minimum Standards for Criminal Justice, Standards Relating to Pleas of Guilty* 1–5 (1968).

at the moment he ordered her into the bedroom, footsteps were heard, he snatched the watch from her wrist and fled. The victim went to phone from a neighbor's apartment—and Townes, during her absence, re-entered her apartment, She screamed on returning and he fled waving a knife—into the arms of waiting police. His prior record included nineteen arrests over a twenty year period, showed an appreciable history of addiction, and embraced at least three prior reduced felonies. Charged with robbery in the first degree and cognate crimes (and so subject to imprisonment for a minimum of ten years and a maximum of thirty), he, too, was permitted to plead guilty to attempted grand larceny in the second degree, as a first felony offender; the maximum term under that plea was one of two-and-a-half years in State's prison. His sentence, in fact, was one of fifteen months to two-and-a-half years, making him eligible for release in about ten months, less credit for time served while awaiting disposition of the charges.'[1]

In a recent year in New York, about 20 per cent of the indictments for armed or other aggravated robberies, for which the minimum punishment is 10 years and the maximum 30 years in state prison, resulted in accepting pleas of guilty to misdemeanors. These are ordinarily punishable by no more than one year in jail. About three quarters of the indictments for aggravated assaults, carrying up to five years of imprisonment, also resulted in pleas of guilty to misdemeanors. Some plea bargaining is the consequence of Draconian laws mandating punishments far beyond anything that is sensible either in terms of community protection or the rehabilitation of offenders. Humane prosecutors understandably refuse to go along with these laws, and, in order to make the punishment fit the crime and the criminal, accept pleas to lesser offenses. Most plea bargaining, however, is not based upon considerations of community safety or the rehabilitation of individual offenders, but upon crowded calendars in the courts and the necessity of disposing of a vast volume of cases without trial. Yet it is taken for granted by all concerned, even when its effect is to divest courts of much of their responsibility and transfer it to the offices of district attorneys.[2]

[1] R. H. Kuh, 'Plea Copping', 24 N.Y. County B. Bull. 160 (1967).
[2] Kuh, *supra*, at 161.

Having learned about plea bargaining, you might be stimulated to see another courtroom where sentencing was being done. The scene would not be much different. The judge would be considering reports by probation officers as to the backgrounds of defendants and the likelihood of their rehabilitation, and possibly also hearing recommendations by assistant district attorneys, which normally would be consistent with promises earlier made to defendants in earlier plea negotiations. Confronted by these two sets of outside recommendations, the judge might be tempted to abdicate his own responsibility for proper sentences, and, in effect, to leave the vital decisions to non-judicial agencies. Whether he abdicated responsibility or not, he would act quickly, because his sentencing calendar might run to 30 or 40 cases for a single morning or afternoon.

I realize that appearances may be deceiving. Perhaps the cases are receiving all the time and attention they deserve. Perhaps the judge who is sentencing offenders has already studied their presentence reports and made up his mind. Perhaps the judges handling arraignments and summary trials can learn all they need to know in a minute or two per case. Perhaps the rights of defendants are being adequately protected, and perhaps each is getting the treatment he deserves. Nevertheless, I cannot help but think of the famous remark of one of the English judges who said: 'Justice must not only be done, it must be seen to be done.' American courts are falling far short of that standard.

Having observed the three examples of assembly line justice that I have described, you might be in the mood to see the judicial process operating under less pressure of time. In that event, you could walk down the corridor again and go into a courtroom where a trial was in progress. The pace would be leisurely, especially if the case was a notorious one, well publicized. The trial would probably already have been postponed several times at the request of the defense counsel or the prosecuting attorney or both. A jury would be in attendance; the lawyers would be arguing rules of evidence; and in general, most of the causes of delay I have been discussing would be at work. The contrast

G

between leisurely trials and hurried arraignments was well summarized in these words by a judge in California:

> 'We are willing to allow a judge and a jury a full week to try a drunk-driving case (involving an heiress) on the theory that a person is entitled to his day in court, and yet at the same time in the drunk-driving arraignment court where the defendants practically all plead guilty, after they have pleaded guilty their cases are handled in a matter of minutes or seconds. It is, of course, important that people have trials in which their rights are fully protected but it is also important that proceedings in the arraignment court should be given adequate time.'[1]

The situation is even worse than the judge indicates. Many men who should be arrested are not, because the police know that the courts cannot process their cases. Many men who have been arrested and who should be brought to trial are either released outright without being arraigned or allowed to plead to less serious offenses than those of which they are guilty for the same reason: prosecutors know that their cases would never be reached.

The New York scenes I have been describing could be duplicated in almost any large city in the United States. Here is the way the picture looks in Los Angeles as described by a judge who had himself been handling misdemeanor arraignments:

> 'In Divisions 50, 58, and 59, defendants are informed of their constitutional rights in crowds ranging in size from 100 to 300 defendants. In Divisions 58 and 59, there are no seats available for the defendants, and they are crowded into a small space between the counsel table and the courtroom seats, in conditions similar to those of New Yorkers crowded in a subway during the rush hour. . . .

> 'To facilitate the arraignment process, bailiffs are obliged to line up the defendants in long lines, blocking up the aisles of the courtroom. As the names of individual defendants are called off, each defendant moves up in the line, shepherded ahead by the bailiffs. . . . By the time the defendant appears before the judge, frequently his only objective is to get out of the courtroom as fast as possible. . . . Under such conditions, it is possible that defendants plead guilty without adequate knowledge of the charges against

[1] R. Clifton, Letter to E. Barrett, Jr. (*Criminal Justice, supra,* p. 79, n. 1, at 122).

them. . . . A plea of guilty under such circumstances does not create respect for the law enforcement process. It certainly does not create a climate for the education of the defendants.'[1]

Here is what the President's Commission on Law Enforcement and the Administration of Justice, which had been studying urban criminal courts throughout the nation, and finding many of them in a state of near collapse, said in 1967:

> 'The Commission has been shocked by what it has seen in some lower courts. It has seen cramped and noisy courtrooms, undignified and perfunctory procedures, and badly trained personnel. It has seen dedicated people who are frustrated by huge caseloads, by the lack of opportunity to examine cases carefully, and by the impossibility of devising constructive solutions to the problems of offenders. It has seen assembly line justice.'[2]

The Commission was talking, as I have been, about urban justice rather than rural or small town justice. But most people today live in cities, not in the country. Since our society is already urbanized to a great extent, and becoming more so as each year passes, urban justice is the kind that affects the vast bulk of the population and that sets the tone of justice for the entire society.

Assembly line methods are less prominent in civil litigation than in criminal litigation, but by no means unknown. Pretrial motions are sometimes heard in undigestible batches of 75 to 100 in a single morning. Trial calendars are often called in a courtroom full of lawyers clamoring to be heard as to why their cases should or should not be adjourned. What are called (sometimes with unconscious humor) 'pretrial conferences' are sometimes held as if the judge were conducting an auction, asking each plaintiff what he will take in settlement and each defendant how much he will offer, and then dividing the sum by two and banging his gavel as the case is settled at the middle figure. Judge Botein, former Presiding Justice of the Appellate Division, First Depart-

---

[1] Nutter, 'The Quality of Justice in Misdemeanor Arraignment Courts', 53 J. of Crim. Law, Criminology and Police Science 215–216 (1962).

[2] President's Commission on Law Enforcement and the Administration of Justice, Challenge of Crime, *supra*, p. 60, n. 3, at 128.

ment of New York, confirmed the existence of this type of
assembly line operation in civil cases when he said:

> '[T]he frenzy with which we try to shorten the long line of cases
> shuffling toward trial, when it is accomplished by hard-pressed
> settlements, is highly indecorous and undignified. . . . [I]nstant
> justice, at the trial or pre-trial stage, can never be a consistent
> substitute for a true justice, which requires time for brewing,
> blending and often brooding. In the stark statistics of reducing
> calendar congestion and delay and keeping most of our calendars
> current, we have been reasonably successful in the First Depart-
> ment. But how has this been achieved? Regretably, by converting
> our courthouses into counting houses.'[1]

In spite of the 'instant justice' of which Judge Botein
speaks, civil cases are delayed at least as long as criminal
cases, perhaps much longer on the average. In some cities,
it takes four or five years after a personal injury action is at issue
before it can be reached for trial.[2] This is a chronic condition
which has persisted for years and shows no signs of being
amenable to cure. Mr. John Frank, a distinguished practicing
lawyer of wide experience, surveyed civil delay over the nation
as a whole in a series of recent lectures at the University of
California at Berkeley, and concluded that:

> 'The administration of the law business of the United States is in a
> state of disaster right now. It grows worse, menacing the very
> existence of justice in this country. For all the diligent and creative
> efforts which have gone into improvement, we have come to
> the end of the road on existing programs. There is nothing which
> the profession is seriously ready to accept right now which will
> cure the situation. We have lost the last great recourse in which we
> have put faith, the endless proliferation of judges and courtrooms.'[3]

That assembly line methods of administering justice should
go hand in hand with dilatory methods is not as strange as it
may seem. Such methods derive from court congestion and the
feeling of compulsion it stimulates in judges to take shortcuts

---

[1] As quoted in Mayer, *The Lawyers* 484 (1967).
[2] I. J. A. Calendar Status Studies, *supra*, p. 60, n. 2.
[3] J. P. Frank, *American Law: The Case for Radical Reform* 58 (1969).

wherever possible and to dispose of cases at almost any price. Both methods lead to the same consequences: resentment, dissatisfaction with the law, loss of respect for the courts, alienation of the public, increased lawlessness, more crime, more cases. So the vicious circle revolves and revolves until the United States is now perilously close to a breakdown of law enforcement and a collapse of civil justice. It is not surprising that law and order was one of the crucial issues in the 1968 presidential campaign in the United States.

In describing the malfunctioning of our judicial system, I have been critical of the courts themselves, but must now try to put that criticism in perspective. I do not believe that the courts are the sole or even the primary cause of our difficulties. Some of the blame falls on homes, schools and churches for their failure to teach citizenship and respect for the law. Some falls upon legislative bodies for their failure to provide the courts with adequate personnel and facilities to keep up with the flood of litigation, and for their many other sins of omission and commission, such as their failure to enact adequate gun control legislation, to deal with pressing social evils, and to reform substantive and procedural law in general. Some falls upon politicians who put incompetent judges into office: some upon white racism and black racism; some upon correctional institutions which fail to rehabilitate young first offenders; some upon lawless police officials and the lack of effective means for disciplining them. So I am very far from placing all the blame on the courts. Nevertheless, the courts must bear part of the blame, and the Supreme Court must shoulder its share of responsibility. I do not mean to pass judgment on the fairness of the Supreme Court decisions in the abstract, as if they were rendered in an ideal society where the courts were on top of their work. I mean only to criticize them in the context of the situation that exists, and to call attention to a fact that is often overlooked—namely, that they are one significant factor among others in causing congestion and delay. They have weakened the doctrine of *stare decisis* and, by increasing the uncertainty of litigation, have increased its volume. They have contributed to the feeling that anybody can get away with anything. They have sidetracked criminal trials away from the main issue of guilt or innocence into tangential inquiries as to the correctness of police and prosecution methods. They have increased the number of trials, especially trials by jury, and also the number of appeals. They have sanctioned collateral attacks upon judgments in great volume, and, in so doing, have created a new breed of legal experts in the convict population of our penitentiaries, whose main therapy is thinking up new grounds for such attacks.

These decisions have been made with little or no thought of their effect on congestion and delay in the lower courts. Yet, paradoxically, some of the men who participated in them were acutely aware that congestion and delay existed in very serious form. In 1958, the Honourable Earl Warren, then Chief Justice, said:

> 'Interminable and unjustifiable delays in our courts are today compromising the basic legal rights of countless thousands of Americans and, imperceptibly, corroding the very foundations of government in the United States. Today, because the legal remedies of many of our people can be realized only after they have sallowed with the passage of time, they are mere forms of justice.'[1]

In 1967, about ten years later, he returned to the theme:

> 'In a century which has been characterized by growth and modernization in science, technology and economics, the legal fraternity is still living in the past. We have allowed the mainstream of progress to pass us by. . . . Our failure to act becomes alarming when a competent district judge must admit in testimony before a Senate committee that unless something new and effective is done promptly in the area of judicial research, coordination and management, the rule of law in this nation cannot endure. When justice is denied to any of our citizens because of faulty administration our failure to act becomes inexcusable.'[2]

[1] Warren, 'The Problem of Delay: Task for Bench and Bar Alike', 44 A.B.A.J. 1043 (1958), address to the Assembly of the A.B.A.

[2] Address by Earl Warren to the Annual Meeting of the American Law Institute, May 16, 1967.

Now the Supreme Court has new leadership in the person of Chief Justice Warren E. Burger, appointed and confirmed in 1969. He has long been concerned with judicial administration and has worked effectively toward its improvement. For example, he has been a member of the faculty of the Appellate Judges Seminars mentioned earlier; he has served as Chairman of the Committee formulating Standards for Criminal Justice, also mentioned earlier; and he has been active in the work of the American Bar Association, the Institute of Judicial Administration and similar organizations devoted to improving the administration of justice. Furthermore, he has long been a student (both appreciative and critical) of the working of the courts in England and continental Europe. Under him, it is fair to expect that the Supreme Court may become more conscious of the effect of its own decisions on delay and congestion in the lower federal courts and in the state courts. And because of his position of leadership in the entire profession, the whole effort at improving the administration of justice may be greatly strengthened. This is presaged by three speeches given by him at the American Bar Association meeting in Dallas, Texas in August 1969, calling for improved, more practical legal education, greater attention to correctional problems, and a training program for court administrators.[1] The training program for court administrators is already on the way toward fruition.

Whatever hopes may now be centered on Supreme Court leadership, thus far efforts at improving the administration of justice in the United States have been puny. We have been seeking superficial solutions for deep problems. We have added new judges, simplified court structures, developed new procedures (like split trials, pretrial conferences and arbitration of small claims), eliminated American style justices of the peace, given procedural rule making power to the courts and the like. These and similar reforms have been worth making; without them, the situation might be worse than it is. But we have not solved the

[1] Burger, 'Court Administrators—Where Would We Find Them?' 53 Judicature 108 (1969).

problems of congestion and delay. We have not attacked their root causes. To men from Mars, or indeed even to Englishmen, we must look like doctors who have been prescribing aspirin for cancer.

The year of the moon shot is no time for the legal profession to comfort itself that it is doing all that needs to be done in judicial administration. It takes longer to get an answer from a defendant in a routine civil case than it takes to send men to the moon and bring them back. It takes longer than a moonshot to produce a decision on a routine appeal—even one that raises no real problems.

The entire space program was conceived and carried out in less time than is consumed in processing dozens upon dozens of run-of-the-mill civil and criminal cases to their final conclusion. Since the beginning of that program, we have added many hundreds of judges to the courts of this nation. Yet our calendars are as far behind as they ever were, if not more so. Meanwhile, our courts have been losing rather than gaining public confidence and respect, and our society has become less orderly, less lawful, less secure than it was before. In short, the situation is deteriorating rather than improving.

Clearly what is needed in the law is the kind of bold, imaginative, radical thinking that has characterized the space program. I hope and believe that we are now beginning to seek bolder solutions. We are becoming more aware than ever before of the magnitude and seriousness of our difficulties. We are beginning to realize that judicial administration is not just a specialized interest of judges and lawyers, but something vital to our whole civilization. The Safe Streets Act passed by Congress in 1968 is a significant piece of legislation and a long step in the right direction. In addition to making a small start toward federal control of traffic in firearms and attempting to counteract some Supreme Court decisions which the Congress considered erroneous, the Act makes available substantial amounts of federal money in the form of grants in aid to states and local communities to improve their systems of criminal justice. A modicum of central control is provided in the sense that state and local plans for improvement must be approved in Washington before substantial amounts of federal money become available. The preamble of the Act is such an eloquent description of present ills and future hopes that it bears repetition:

'Congress finds that the high incidence of crime in the United States threatens the peace, security, and general welfare of the Nation and its citizens. To prevent crime and to ensure the greater safety of the people, law enforcement efforts must be better coordinated, intensified, and made more effective at all levels of government.

'Congress finds further that crime is essentially a local problem that must be dealt with by State and local governments if it is to be controlled effectively.

'It is therefore the declared policy of the Congress to assist State and local governments in strengthening and improving law enforcement at every level by national assistance. It is the purpose of this title to (1) encourage States and units of general local government to prepare and adopt comprehensive plans based upon their evaluation of State and local problems of law enforcement; (2) authorize grants to States and units of local government in order to improve and strengthen law enforcement; and (3) encourage research and development directed toward the improvement of law enforcement and the development of new methods for the prevention and reduction of crime and the detection and apprehension of criminals.'[1]

At the present time there is no civil equivalent to the Safe Streets Act. It is just as badly needed, because civil justice is no better than criminal justice. However, some help in a limited way may be found in an act passed by Congress in 1967 establishing the Federal Judicial Center as a research arm for the federal courts.[2] If it develops the courage, vision and resources to successfully tackle congestion and delay in civil cases in the federal courts,

[1] Pub. L. 90–351, June 19, 1968, 82 Stat. 197.
[2] 28 U.S.C. § 620 (1964) (Supp. III 1968), Pub. L. 90–219, title I § 101, Dec. 20, 1967, 81 Stat. 664; See also, Clark, 'The New Federal Judicial Center', 54 A.B.A.J. 743 (1968).

it may also set the pattern for dealing with those problems in the state courts.

Because of these and similar developments in the states, as well as others described earlier, such as the promulgation of Standards of Criminal Justice, I can end this grim chapter, and indeed this entire book, on an affirmative, hopeful note. Responsible leaders of the bench, the bar and the general public are more conscious than they ever have been before of the appalling conditions in our courts. They are beginning to raise their voices in a growing chorus of protest. Perhaps this presages a full-scale, all-out attack on the fundamental causes of congestion and delay in both civil and criminal cases, in state as well as federal courts. Such an attack involves more than action by the courts alone. It involves major legislative and constitutional changes, changes in education, and in professional and public attitudes.

Quaere whether there is any other alternative if the rule of law is to survive in America? Quaere further whether our civilization itself can survive if the rule of law fails?

Index